Preface

The artistic career of Kurt Thomas is part of an illustrious heritage. Among those honored as Johann Sebastian Bach's successors at St. Thomas's in Leipzig, he was the first to be appointed cantor, in 1957, because of his stature as a composer of choral music. With his Mass for double chorus, *a cappella* Op. 1—dedicated, like the *Hymni Sacri* of Seth Calvisius, the *Opella Nova* of Johann Hermann Schein, and the *Geistliche Chormusik* of Heinrich Schütz, to the choir at St. Thomas's—the twenty-one-year-old Kurt Thomas startled many, in the era of musical Expressionism, with a novel style which marked the beginning of a fresh choral literature and influenced Johann Nepomuk David, Ernst Pepping, Hugo Distler, and a number of other choral composers.

The decisive implementation of this reinvigorated *a cappella* practice, however, came by means of his work as a choral conductor. After being appointed lecturer to the faculty of the Leipzig Conservatory in 1925, Thomas, a student of Karl Straube, established in the immediate vicinity of the Thomaskirche a new style of choral performance. With his *Kantorei,* a chamber chorus formed mainly of his conducting students, he traveled throughout the Continent. Continuing his work at the State Academy in Berlin, where he was appointed professor of composition and choral conducting at the age of thirty, he trained virtually a generation of choral conductors. In 1939 he founded the Musische Gymnasium in Frankfort as a counterpart to the Leipzig Thomasschule.

There have been numerous editions and translations, including one in Japanese, of Thomas's *Lehrbuch der Chorleitung,* which was first published in 1935. The present version is the first to appear in English. Based on the author's conducting classes, the book is designed to serve both the beginning and the experienced student of choral conducting: in addition to a systematic course, it contains a wealth of suggestions and observations intended to confirm or modify technical, pedagogical, and stylistic details with which the professional conductor deals daily.

With the exception of the activity of Eberhard Schwickerath as a conductor and writer, to which Thomas refers, there had been actually no formulation of a choral method when Thomas began his work. The excellent collection of *Chorübungen* by Franz Wuellner, which had been published without instruction for the choral conductor, was expanded by Schwickerath in a new edition that contained a discussion of basic choral problems. The *Lehrbuch* is directed toward the *a cappella* situation, and is based on the premise that none of the refinements of *a cappella* training should be lost when chorus and orchestra are combined. (In two supplementary volumes the author deals with special aspects of advanced conducting technique—such as the treatment of recitative—and with the question of the choirmaster's orchestral practice.)

Thomas was primarily concerned with the problem that a professional image for the choral conductor was not as yet established, but it was precisely the established conductor of the symphonic repertoire who lacked the professional experience of handling a chorus. The fact that the choral conductor, unlike his orchestral colleague, is likely to work with nonprofessionals was never accepted by the author as a valid argument. A guiding thought for his work was his formulation of the choral conductor's unusual educational challenge: "There are no bad choruses—only bad choral conductors."

In preparing this translation of the *Lehrbuch* it has been necessary to adapt the examples and the style of presentation to comply with current choral practice in English-speaking countries. The translators have assumed this task on the basis of close acquaintance with the author's work both as students in his conducting classes in Berlin and as hosts to various courses given under his direction in the United States. The English edition is presented to new groups of readers in the hope that they may benefit as much as others have in the past, and it is dedicated to the author as *Festgabe* on the occasion of his sixty-fifth birthday.

ALFRED MANN
WILLIAM H. REESE

KURT THOMAS

The Choral Conductor

The Technique of Choral Conducting in Theory and Practice

English Adaptation by
ALFRED MANN
and
WILLIAM H. REESE

By arrangement with the publishers of|Kurt Thomas's Lehrbuch der Chorleitung.
Breitkopf and Härtel, Weisbaden.

Associated Music Publishers

New York/London

© Copyright 1971 by Associated Music Publishers, Inc., New York
AMP-7005   All Rights Reserved   Printed in U.S.A.
ISBN 0–911320–93–8
Library of Congress Catalog Card No. 70–146229

CONTENTS

CHAPTER 1

Qualifications and Basic Technique

In considering the qualifications for choral conducting it is important to distinguish between those based on natural ability, which can be cultivated to a certain extent but not acquired, and those based on an ability which is acquired through intensive study and practice.

Natural Ability

A fine sense of intonation is extremely important for the choral conductor. Absolute pitch is not a requisite, as is demonstrated by the many eminent musicians who lack it, with obviously no detriment to their professional competence. Absolute pitch may, in fact, turn out to be a disadvantage in the matter of transposition, often needed in dealing with works of the 16th and 17th centuries, or with problems of intonation (although these problems can, of course, be overcome through conscientious work). In any event, the sense of absolute pitch could only rarely be applied to adjust intonation. More likely than not, deviations from the proper pitch would be registered when the borderline of the quarter-tone has been passed —that is, when it is too late. However, every student of choral conducting should have a sure sense of relative pitch and cultivate it to the highest degree.

Another natural ability which is required is the ability of communicating ideas—a critical aspect of conducting. Further requirements are the ability to speak before a group, considerable organizational talent, and psychological sensitivity.

However, the most important requisites are patience and a calm disposition (which is not to be confused with lack of temperament!). No matter how much the conductor's nerves may be strained through working with the choir, they must not give way; nor must they give way under the strain of organizational tasks preceding a concert. The slightest nervousness or lack of concentration will be sensed by the choir. There should be no harsh or impatient word spoken during rehearsal. No one can sing if the joy and ease are taken out of singing. Yet it is precisely in this respect that many choral conductors fail.

1

Qualifications That Can Be Acquired

What are the requisites for choral conducting that can be acquired? "Every choral conductor must be an accomplished musician, a trained singer as well as a trained speaker," says Eberhard Schwickerath, one of the few conductors who achieved outstanding results at the turn of the century when choral work was at its lowest ebb.[1]

It is imperative that a choral conductor have some vocal training. The potential of his own voice is obviously a secondary consideration. But only if he himself masters the technical and expressive aspects of singing, and is able to demonstrate all fine points or details pertaining to tone and diction, can he expect the same from his choir. Every choir sings and enunciates like its conductor.

Of great importance to a choral conductor is his own experience of singing in well-directed choruses—preferably at a time when he is in charge of his own choir. Besides solidifying his knowledge of the literature, his own participation will help him understand better the psychological make-up of the choir, and the various influences to which the choir is subject—in short, he will study the perspective from which he is seen.

In addition, the choral conductor must be well versed in music theory; he must have a command of harmony, counterpoint, and form. He must be equally well versed in music history, especially in the development of choral literature: he must be well acquainted with the styles and performance practices of different periods. If necessary, the young conductor should pursue concurrent studies in these areas while he is studying conducting.

It is desirable that the choral conductor know some Latin, Italian, and German—"not only should he know that *Deus* means 'God,' that *sanctus* means 'holy,' that *miserere nobis* means 'have mercy on us': he must think and feel in the language," says Schwickerath in the work quoted above. The choral conductor must be a capable performer on one or several instruments and be able to play from score. Finally, the most essential qualification among those that can be acquired is manual dexterity—the basis of the technique of conducting to which the next section will be devoted.

Importance of Technique

In addition to setting and keeping time, conducting technique should remind the chorus at the crucial moment of all that has been practiced and achieved in rehearsals. Not only must conducting convey clarity of rhythm, entrances, and direction in general, but it must also convey expressive qualities, interpretation of the text, subtleties of intonation and other technical aspects of performance.

In spite of the many problems involved, all conducting motions must be clear and simple and as economical as possible. Any choir, even the

[1] *Chorübungen* (Munich, 1931), p. 229.

largest, can be trained to follow very small motions. In short, the success of the conductor will depend upon using *only* those gestures that a convincing interpretation demands. Even the smallest motion must have meaning and purpose.

A thorough understanding of the technique of conducting is obviously of the greatest importance to the choral conductor: lack of technique might invalidate much that has been gained in painstaking rehearsal work. Only a conducting technique of the first rank and equal to all the complexities of modern rhythm (the works of the old masters, too, abound in rhythmic complexity) can support what has been achieved in rehearsal and lead to perfect performance.

General Remarks on Posture

The importance of posture in conducting should not be underestimated. Nothing must disturb the chorus or audience in concentrating on what is most essential—the music. Such concentration is best accomplished by doing away not only with all ungainly motions, but also with "beautiful" motions which are used for the audience.

The conductor's stance should be natural. His feet should be fairly close together—a slight separation will help to achieve a relaxed position. To place the feet far apart would suggest an attitude of tenseness, as would a distorted facial expression. Any controlled, desirable tension must be the result of complete relaxation—the point of departure for all study and practice of conducting technique.

The entire body should reflect freedom and elasticity. From this it follows that *both* arms must be equally involved in conducting. Conducting with only one hand is at times required in rehearsal but is not feasible in actual performance. Obviously both arms should not just move symmetrically; but as long as a lack of technique precludes perfected individual motions for each arm, it will be better to let both of them do the same thing (moving, of course, to opposite sides) than to arrest the motion of one arm, and let it hang down—or place it on the hip. Such "one-sided" conducting gives the other side of the body a paralyzed appearance and can never lead to free, unconstrained singing.

Generally, the upper part of the body should remain still. In giving an entrance to a particular section no more than a slight turn of the upper body is needed (a turn of just the head or the eyes would give a very awkward and stiff impression). Likewise, a slight backward motion of the upper part of the body might be used to indicate decreasing intensity, and a slight forward motion to indicate increasing intensity. The position of the upper body, the manner of holding the head, the expression of the eyes should all express complete freedom. When looking at the chorus, the conductor should always appear in control, helping and encouraging. He should know the score by heart or refer to it with only an occasional glance.

Freedom must also be expressed in the position of the arms and the hands to the fingertips. Freedom and relaxed resilience must be expressed by the entire body. To repeat: the technique of conducting can to a large extent be acquired through study. In my opinion, unsurmountable physical difficulties are only rarely encountered. Experience has shown that precisely those who approach this study with some tenseness may eventually achieve good results, because any conscious struggle against inner or outer obstacles is bound to produce intensified strength. Those to whom everything comes naturally and without intensive work will, more often than not, show disappointing results in the end. Perfection—which is all too rare—is the result of natural gift and hard work.

Conducting Without Baton

One thing should be understood above all: a mastery of technique is not the goal but the first requirement for the art of conducting—the art of suggesting the expressive nuances of music and text. To do justice to the full range of expressive possibilities of *a cappella* performance, *both hands* should be *free*. This is why I reject the baton.

The argument that conducting with "bare" hands lacks precision is based on prejudice; it is just as possible to give an inaccurate beat *with* the baton as an accurate beat *without* it. The determining factor is rather who gives the beat and on what his experience is based. I have often found that students who at first reject the idea of working without the baton eventually reject the baton.

"I have never used a baton in *a cappella* work, even with a very large number of singers. Arms, hands, and fingers can suggest matters of tone production, phrasing, diction, and complexities of rhythm more clearly than the baton," says Schwickerath in the work previously mentioned.[2] (One can imagine the effect this unorthodox approach to conducting must have had among "specialists" of his day.) But for his choirs, this approach became a *conditio sine qua non:* those who experience the expressive powers of a conducting technique using both hands become averse to watching the baton, which of necessity deadens the live expression of one hand. Schwickerath's innovation found a following only decades later in a younger generation. Today this following is obvious and widespread.

Conducting without baton has been adopted by orchestral conductors in many countries. Even where very large choral and instrumental performance forces are involved, conducting without baton has proved its effectiveness. The objection of insufficient visibility at great distances defeats itself; actually the hands are more clearly visible than a thin baton. I am sure that the use of the baton will gradually disappear, although I do not want to make this point a cardinal issue. Time will indeed decide.

For the purposes of study, however, I rule out the use of the baton. It

---

[2] *Chorübungen*, p. 233.

is easy to change to the baton later when the orchestra enters the picture. But it is difficult, if not impossible, ever to conduct without a baton, if the expressive possibilities of the right hand are forfeited at the outset.

The Preparatory Posture

What should precede the first beat and its preparatory beat? I call this the preparatory posture or position—a position which should establish concentration as well as visual contact between the conductor and each member of the choir. The preparatory posture should also anticipate the character and expressive quality of the work about to be performed.

Keeping in mind the equal involvement of both arms, the proper placing of the hands in the preparatory posture is easily determined: the upper arms should be raised to a horizontal position and the lower arms should be held loosely in front of the chest (at a distance of 5 to 10 inches from the body, depending upon the intensity of the first entrance).

This preparatory or normal posture, in which the shoulders should be invariably relaxed and the elbows slightly pushed out, will form a central position around which all motions revolve and from which there is a possibility of executing beats in all directions—up, down, sideways, toward or away from the body. The more one keeps within this normal, central position, and limits the use of highly intensified gestures (placed forward) or decidedly reduced gestures (placed closer to the body), the greater will be their effect.

As I have mentioned, various degrees of intensity should be expressed through the preparatory posture: a high degree of intensity, to prepare for a strongly marked and forceful entrance, by placing the hands at some distance from the body; relative relaxation, to prepare for an entrance of medium expressive and dynamic strength, by holding the hands closer to the body; and gentleness, by a subduing gesture of the hands quite close to the body. In addition, the height at which the hands are placed in the preparatory posture will depend upon the beat on which the preparation of the entrance must occur. If the preparatory beat is downward, the hands must naturally be placed somewhat higher; if it is toward the center, the hands must be farther apart; if it is upward, the hands must be lower, etc. The height at which the hands are placed also depends upon the position of the choir and conductor: if the conductor is placed very high, the position of the hands should be lower than indicated; if he is placed low, the position of the hands will have to be considerably higher for clear visibility. Finally, the conductor's physical height should be taken into consideration and may very well require certain deviations from the normal preparatory posture we have described.

Aside from the general placement, the specific position of the hands and fingers also depends on the expressive quality of the work. Tension is best suggested by placing thumb and forefinger loosely together; the other fingers should be slightly but not stiffly separated.

Table Ia

Table Ib

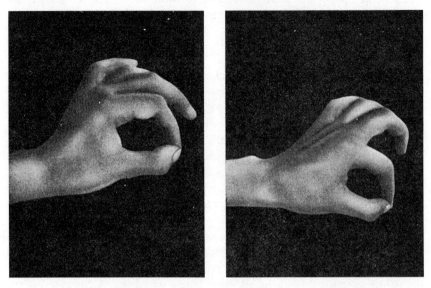

Correct

Exaggerated

An entrance of medium strength is best prepared by holding the hands in a normally relaxed manner, not in a weak one, which would be suggested if the fingers are rolled in.

Table IIa

Table IIb

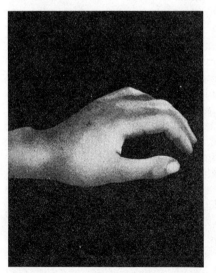

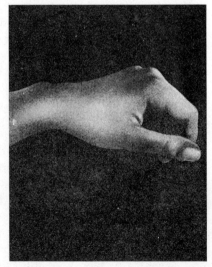

Correct

Too weak

Soft and subdued entrances should be anticipated by a more opened position of the hands and a gentle outward turn of the palms.

Table III

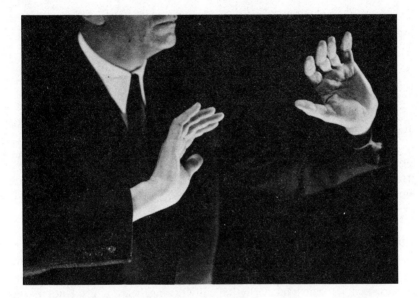

The duration of the preparatory posture is determined by the amount of time needed for the choir—and the audience—to reach the highest point of concentration. At this moment the preparatory beat for the entrance should occur, and not a moment later; otherwise the intensity of concentration will decrease, and it becomes necessary to wait for another high point. Some experience is necessary properly to judge the exact moment, but this will be easily recognized by a sensitive conductor.

The Preparatory Beat

The problem of the preparatory beat is similar to that of the preparatory posture which precedes it; the entrance requires a decisive preparatory beat with which the tempo is set and from which the dynamic and expressive character of the piece can be clearly recognized. At the same time, the preparatory beat—during which the conductor should inhale—must compellingly suggest inhaling to the choir. The preparation must be so clear that at the moment of the entrance itself the conducting motion could stop without the slighest change of tempo resulting.

There are two kinds of preparatory beats: one that serves for the preparation of an entrance on the beat,

Ex. 1

Ma - to - na, love - ly maid - en, oh, lis - ten to __ the song,
Ma - to - na, mi - a ca - ra, mi fol - le - re __ can - zon,

and one that serves for the preparation of an entrance occurring between two beats of a measure.

Ex. 2

Thou gen - tle heart, how dear thou art,
Dein Herz - lein mild, du lie - bes Bild,

In the first instance, the beat preceding that on which the entrance occurs must be indicated in the preparatory motion. If a piece written in 4/4 begins on the fourth beat, the third quarter will be indicated. If the piece is in 2/2 and begins on "one," the second half-note of an imaginary preceding measure should be indicated as a preparatory beat. If the piece is in 6/8 and begins on beat "five," the fourth eighth should be indicated, etc. As mentioned above, the preparatory motion must be absolutely clear. However, if it occurs on a rhythmically strong beat, it need not be very large.

In the second case—the entrance occurring between two beats of the measure—the first of these two beats must be strongly indicated in the preparatory motion. The entrance will then follow without further help, or merely be supported by a glance, or a slight motion of the head, or, if necessary, a subdivision of the beat through the wrist.

Under no circumstances should the preparatory motion be preceded by any other motion—a preparation for the preparation, which could go on ad infinitum. The preparatory beat must be given from a preparatory motionless posture.

The Entrance

The preparatory beat is immediately followed by the entrance. Up to this point eye contact between conductor and chorus must be maintained without fail. Since it is impossible to look at everyone simultaneously, eye contact with the entire chorus should be gradually established during the preparatory position. Then the conductor should glance to *one* side of the chorus during the preparatory beat and to the *other* side at the moment of the entrance. These matters will in time become second nature to a conductor but at the beginning must be done consciously.

The Different Meters

The conducting motions for all types of meter have the following in common: the first and strongest beat of the measure leads downward, following the law of gravity, and the beat next in importance—"two" in 3/4 or 3/2 meter; "three" in 4/8, 4/4, or 4/2; and "four" in 6/8, 6/4, or 6/2—leads outward, to be plainly visible.

From the schematic drawings (see Fig. 1), which show the succession of beats for the principal metric patterns, it will be seen that each beat, as well as indicating its main direction, must also include a small downward motion. The validity of each beat is precisely at the point where the line is most heavily marked. It is here that the beat attains its greatest speed and intensity. The curve that follows in each case is to be considered a release leading to the next beat. I have gradually come to realize the necessity of letting each beat drop vertically to its point of validity. One should imagine three levels: the first level for the beat of "one," a second and somewhat higher level for all other beats except the last, and a third and highest for the last beat. The point of validity for each beat is fixed by the touching of, and bouncing back from, the respective levels.

Figure 1a

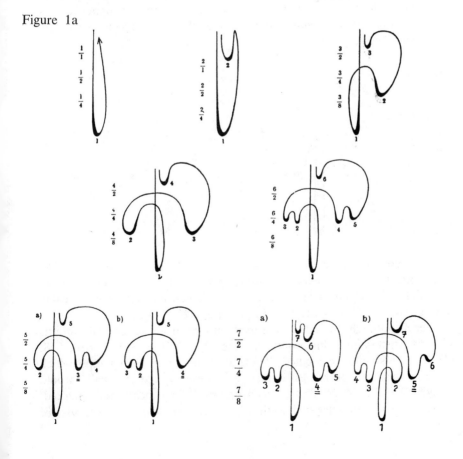

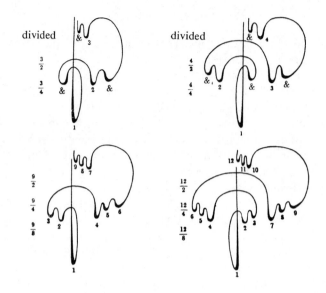

The release of any beat after the point of validity should not take the direction of the beat that follows but rather the direction opposite to it (see Fig. 1a). In this manner the focus of the following beat will gain additional clarity.

Figure 1b

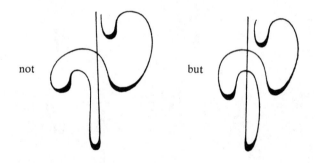

All meters can be conducted to connote two types of expression: (1) a rhythmically oriented manner, through motions that are rapid, accentuated, and resilient; and (2) a melodically oriented manner, through calm, flowing motions very lightly marking the point of validity.

After a thorough practice of the examples given above, special patterns related to meters involving groups of three (3/2, 3/4, 3/8; 6/2, 6/4, 6/8; 9/8; 12/8) should be studied. These patterns apply to a tempo which would be rendered too restless if every beat were marked, but which would be indistinct if only the first in each group of three beats were marked. There are many examples such as the 12/8 meter in the opening choruses of

Bach's *St. Matthew Passion* and of the second part of the *Christmas Oratorio*.

The special execution of these triple meter patterns lies in the fact that the first beat of each group does not immediately bounce back but comes to a halt at its lowest point. Only after this halt does the first beat bounce into the second beat; in fact, the release of beat "one" leads to a second halt which must be reached precisely at the point of validity of beat "two." Finally, beat "three" is executed and immediately released in the usual manner.

In Figs. 2a, b, c, d, the halting points are indicated by circles, and the points of validity are indicated, as before, by the thick portions of the lines. In 3/2, 3/4 or 3/8 meter the conducting figure shows the following "cone" shape:

Figure 2a

In the compound patterns, this shape is varied through the changed direction of the third beat within each group of three. The variants produce figures which, taken as complete units, suggest the basic figures of duple, triple, and quadruple meter (Figs. 2b, c, d).

Figure 2b   Figure 2c   Figure 2d

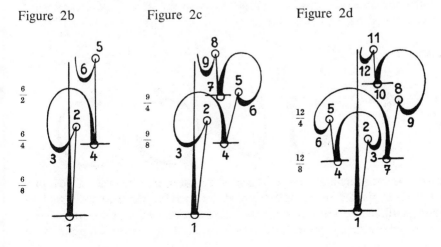

The best way to describe the special motion required in these conducting patterns might be to suggest the overcoming of a considerable resistance, such as the tension of a strong spring working against gravity. Thus the downward motion calls for an intense use of the arm muscles, possibly supported by a slight motion of the body. The release occurs immediately before "two," as if the pull of the imaginary spring were taking effect, carrying the hands with great speed to the upper halting point precisely on "two."

The Cut-off

Only in the case of a fermata does the cut-off present a special conducting problem. On a caesura or a close without fermata, the cut-off is executed like any other beat. The fermata, which indicates a logical, though arbitrary rhythmic variance (the idea that the fermata lengthens a note by half its value is a fairy tale!), poses greater problems in choral than orchestral performance because correct diction for different word endings must be considered. Remember that a fermata can properly begin only at the point where all voices have reached their final note; at times composers fail to exercise care in their notation and place fermatas at different places in different voices.

It is of primary importance that the moment at which the fermata ends be precisely marked. A clearly visible point should be chosen for the required motion, preferably at the level of the preparatory position. A lower position may not be clearly visible; a higher position may look awkward. A cut-off without release is entirely wrong (see Fig. 3a). An ending *t*, for instance, could never be made to sound together in this manner. Equally impractical are the often-used figures of circle or curve (see Figs. 3b, c). A circle, having neither end nor beginning, is particularly unsuited for indicating an ending: the final point of the motion cannot be determined. The number of conductors showing a predilection for the use of these conducting figures is inversely proportional to the number of clear final *t* sounds heard by their audiences.

Figure 3

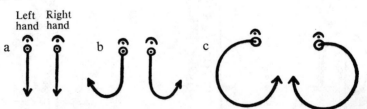

It may seem difficult at first to adjust to the manner of fermata conducting which is explained in the following. But I have found repeatedly that in spite of initial doubt students used to other methods adopt this one quickly.

The conducting motion on the fermata itself is a problem peculiar to choral conducting. In conducting an orchestra, one might possibly hold the hands in one position until the beat is cut off, but in conducting a choir, the beat on which the fermata falls should be conducted with the usual release into the normal position. From this point on, however, I recommend a gradual raising of the hands, well calculated to last for the duration of the fermata and leading to the point from which the cut-off is given. This raising of the hands has some advantages: it will prevent flatting or loss of intensity of tone (if a decreasing sound is intended, it should be expressed through the cautioning turning of the palms shown in Table 3), and more space is gained for the cut-off beat.

The highest point of the upward motion should be determined by the dynamic strength of the final chord, but it should not be higher than the conductor's head. From this highest point the cut-off beat is performed quickly, moving both hands down, and preferably somewhat out. Immediately after this, the motion bounces back to the normal position in which the hands, almost meeting, come to rest.

Figure 4

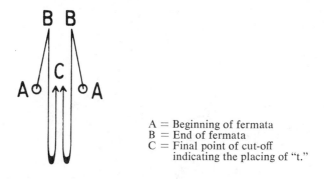

A = Beginning of fermata
B = End of fermata
C = Final point of cut-off
    indicating the placing of "t."

For fermata cut-offs ending with a sharp *t,* there should be an almost vertical motion downward and bouncing up again. (This obviously cannot be shown in a schematic drawing since the stroke showing one direction would cover the other.) The speed of the cut-off beat and its release and the extent of the entire motion will again depend upon the intensity of the final chord, and will also depend upon the final consonant.

If the fermata is followed by a new entrance, the cut-off will have to be placed so that it can serve as a preparatory beat for this new entrance—unless there is a definite break and time for an actual pause between the cut-off and the new entrance.

At the conclusion of an entire work one should hold the normal posture for a short time to allow for a moment of reflection. Nothing is more distasteful than the immediate transition to the noise and trouble of everyday life. The listener wants time to collect his thoughts. But if the conductor does not express an attitude of absorption, and contentedly drops his arms once the last tone is sounded, the choir cannot be expected to maintain its concentration in turn. The actual conclusion, then, should be a moment's pause—short or long, depending upon the nature of the work—in the normal position. Thus the cycle from beginning to end will be logically completed in thought and motion.

A voiceless consonant occurring at the end must be deliberately anticipated by the conductor so that the singers can prepare for it. This preparation coincides with the downward motion. The consonant itself—using *t* again as the example—is pronounced precisely at the moment that the choir can understand as the final moment of motion: the return of the hands to the resting position. The very unsatisfactory but all too frequent involuntary staggering of a final *t,* or the situation in which it is timidly suppressed, can surely be avoided by clear conducting.

A vowel occurring at the end should be treated in a similar manner. On the other hand, a voiced consonant will require more time than can be indicated by a precise cut-off, especially if it follows an extended, broadly reverberating hold. In that case the concluding beat will lead through a small detour (during which a consonant such as the *n* will be sounded) and then back to the normal position (see Fig. 5).

Figure 5

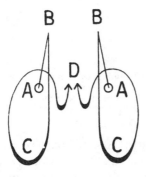

A = Start of fermata
B = Conclusion of fermata
C = Start of the consonant
D = Conclusion of the consonant

As can be seen in Figure 5, there are actually two motions to be performed. One leads to the other, yet each has its own release: one for the end of the fermata and the other for the end of the liquescent consonant. If this delayed fermata cut-off is too difficult, a motion similar to the precise fermata cut-off could be used. In that case, the cut-off motion must be performed rather slowly; the wrist should be allowed to hang down when the lowest point of the motion is reached, and it must return to the normal position by a motion that is again quite deliberate.

A special difficulty arises when both types of endings are combined—for instance in a word ending on *nd.* Here the second type applies, so that the *n* may be sufficiently heard. But at the last moment the use of a small precise finger motion will be advisable to indicate the *d.*

Table IVa   Table IVb

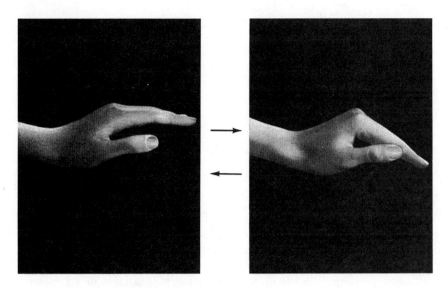

It is unnecessary to point out that the schemes given in Figures 4 and 5 represent extreme situations, such as a strongly pronounced *t* in a *forte* ending or a gently extended *n* in a *piano* ending. Smaller or less intense motions appropriate for situations that involve a smaller dynamic range or final sounds of lesser emphasis may easily be derived from the given schemes.

CHAPTER 2

A Practical Course in Conducting

Methods of Study

We will now discuss the practical application of the material presented in Chapter 1. Truly successful practice can begin only when this material has been thoroughly studied and absorbed.

In my experience, the best practice situation is in a class of six to ten participants, one of whom conducts while the others sing and the instructor comments. Individual instruction is possible but it is made difficult by the absence of a choral group—the "instrument" through which the effect of the conducting exercises can be observed. It is most essential that the preparation for course work begin with memorizing the examples. For individual practice the use of a mirror is strongly recommended, so that the effect of conducting motions can be observed to some degree. In this manner the study of choral conducting can be guided by self-instruction, but eventually the need for a directing and controlling influence will be felt.

The larger the number of participants the more the emphasis should be given to exercises that can be done by the entire group. Even a class of fifty can achieve technical progress; however, this is obviously not an ideal situation.

Practice of Different Meters

The schemes of metric patterns shown on page 9 should be used as the first exercises. Standing before the class, the instructor should let the members imitate him in large flowing motions (always with both arms). This might be done most effectively with unison singing of familiar songs. The motions must be relaxed and come from the shoulders. It is important immediately to alert the student of the bouncing release of each motion. On the whole, choral work requires more of an upward than a downward motion, a continuously lifting, "weightless" beat. This is as essential for a fine choral sound as it is for correct intonation.

A good mental aid is to imagine that the lower arms are suspended by large rubber bands or metal springs that pull them up after each motion; or imagine that each motion is directed upward by magnetic force and that the downward conducting motions counteract such a force. But the force persists and the arms invariably come up again with an intensity in direct proportion to the intensity and speed of their downward motion: each release must correspond in magnitude to its beat. To achieve this elasticity of motion is a great problem, since the adult has lost the natural ease that the child possesses.

Eurhythmic exercises are the only effective remedy. This is not the place to discuss such training in detail, but a few suggestions can be given:

1. Bend forward, let one arm hang down, set it in slight pendular motion and let it come to a complete rest, feeling the full weight of the arm. Repeat with the other arm.

2. Stretch out the arms to the side or to the front, and let them drop with complete relaxation. Swing the entire upper body, raising the arms first above the head, then bringing them down through the spread legs.

3. Bend forward, feet together, knees straight. Move arms toward each other—crossing as they move in opposite directions, but not touching. Let the pendular motion gradually come to a standstill. The shoulders should be completely relaxed.

4. Let both arms hang down, bend forward, push down vigorously, and touch the floor with the fingertips fifteen to twenty-five times. Shoulders and arms should be relaxed.

Such exercises might alternate with the practice of different meters. In addition, the metric patterns should be practiced in two ways: with broadly swinging continuous motions—*legato*—and with quickly stopped bouncing motions—*staccato*. Both patterns should be practiced using larger and smaller motions, the arms moving in opposite directions and describing symmetric patterns. As the arms are brought together, they should be placed one above the other.

To become accustomed to the positions in which the raised arms are held completely still, use a very slow tempo but perform and release each separate motion very quickly within the various metric patterns so that between one beat and the next hands and arms remain motionless. (This is important for a relaxed preparatory position that will nevertheless be effective in conveying concentration and for obtaining a precise beat.) Alternate this exercise again with the eurhythmic exercises described above.

In 4/4 time this type of accented beat produces the following figure:

Figure 6

x = point of validity for each beat

0 = point where release of each beat comes to a standstill

In contrast, the figure for the unaccented continuous beat is as follows:

Figure 7

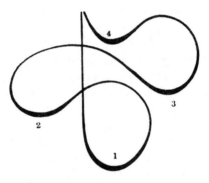

Both represent extreme cases. The normal way of conducting combines the swinging motion of the latter with the fixed beats of the former (approaching each point of validity with slightly increased speed). See Figure 1 on p. 9. All three types must be practiced conscientiously; in fact, both the experienced conductor and the student should use them for regular morning exercises.

The essence of good conducting motions is the constant interchange of tension and relaxation. Strongly fixed and freely swinging beats should be practiced in direct alternation: a quick and immediately released beat "one" may be followed by a completely relaxed beat "two" performed without any visible preparatory readjustment. An aid in obtaining an effective release for each beat is to imagine that the impetus for each motion of the arm comes from the tips of the toes and involves the whole body (but without bending the knees).

Beat "one," as well as any cut-off beat, leads straight down, the release forming an almost complete return straight up—as if guided by rails. (The

2/2 pattern is an exception; similarly, to be visible, the release of "one" is indicated by a slight deviation from a strictly vertical direction in our schematic drawings.) No beat must lead as far down as "one." If this rule is not observed—which unfortunately often happens—the conductor and performers might have uncomfortable misunderstandings, at least in orchestral conducting. (See Figs. 8a and b.)

Figure 8

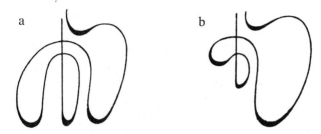

Other less effective though quite widely used examples of conducting figures are:

Figure 9

The motions indicated here are too flat and indistinct to allow for any rhythmic formulation or musical precision. Only in those rare cases where rhythm plays a subordinate role might they be applied to mitigate or counteract undesirable accents. (In general, of course, conducting motions should evoke what is not expressed or insufficiently expressed, and should suppress what is incorrectly or too emphatically expressed.)

Particularly avoid a lack of distinction in executing the last beat within any given metric pattern. Since this beat serves as preparation for beat "one"—the most important beat—it must be specially clarified by a small downward motion (though small it must be precise) and its release (see Fig. 10).

Figure 10

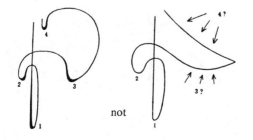

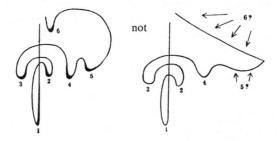

[Note: Beat "two" of the triple subdivision is marked slightly to the right of beat "one," whereas in Fig. 1 it is slightly to the left of beat "one." Actually the two beats might be on the same line, which cannot be shown in our schematic drawing. But all three variants might very well be used: the minor deviation from the vertical beat is not important.]

Another conducting mannerism that should be castigated is the unnecessary elaboration of a beat that results from a backtracking motion. This obscures the basic conducting figure and wastes energy that might be better utilized. "As little movement as possible; as much movement as necessary" should be your motto. This does not stem from laziness but from a sense of economy: the special motion is saved for the special effect.

Figure 11

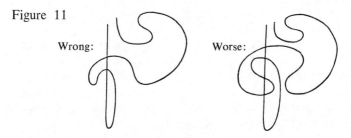

But there *is* one situation where the retracing motion that is normally to be rejected may be used to advantage: it could occasionally lend special stress to one particular beat. Thus it could be applied to the upbeat subdivision of a slow 8/8, 9/8, or 12/8 measure to give clarity and emphasis to the following "one."

Figure 12

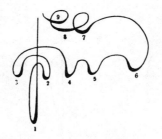

The devising of combinations of various meters as well as transitions from large to small motions (or vice versa) depends on the instructor's imagination. Exercises that should be supported by crisp counting (for motions such as shown in Fig. 6) or by drawn out counting (for motions such as shown in Fig. 7) help immeasurably to enliven the teaching situation. It will also be helpful to change the metric patterns (upon clear announcement) from measure to measure: three-four, six-four, two-four, four-four, five-four with accent on three, two-four, four-four, six-four, five-four with accent on four, three-four, etc.

Also practice changing from arm motion—emanating from the shoulder—to wrist and even finger motion: the point from which the motion originates will simply move from shoulder to wrist or hand. Wrist motions should be sharp and precise, the overall direction of the beat being gently supported by a sideways motion of the lower arm. Finger motions should be similarly executed, the overall direction of the beat being gently supported by a motion of the wrist. Any basic impetus for the conducting motions, however, should come from the shoulder, never from the elbow. Arm and wrist motions should not be employed simultaneously; a dangling, inaccurate beat would be the result.[1]

One of the best ways to gain greater security in executing conducting motions is to alternate hands while changing meters. Although this procedure calls for a high degree of concentration, it might well be tried this early in the course.

The position of the hands should be carefully and constantly checked. The discussion of the position of the hands in the preparatory position (see p. 5) applies to conducting as well. The fingers should be held close enough to suggest that they are invisibly linked from the tip of the thumb to the tip of the little finger. The latter must not be dropped or rolled inwards; either position would suggest a somewhat introverted expression. For a natural flowing beat always use the relaxed position of the hand (Table IIa, p. 6); for a precise, accented beat use the fixed position of the hand (Table Ia, p. 6); for a very light beat use the subduing hand position (Table Va)—as the occasion may demand. Forming a fist, or other

Table Va   Table Vb

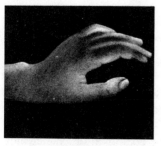

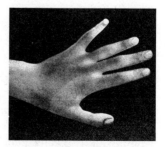

Correct   Exaggerated

[1] An exception is the use of the wrist for subdividing the beat; see p. 25.

hand positions that are apt to smother the tone production, should not be tolerated. By the same token, a stereotyped, expressionless position of the hand should be avoided.

The wrist must remain essentially straight—the thumb forming a direct continuation of the lower arm (see Table VIa). If the hand hangs down (Table VIb), the performance loses clarity and strength; if the hand is forced up, the performance produces a false tension. There should be only slight deviations from—and a smooth return to—the basic straight wrist position.

Table VIa   Table VIb

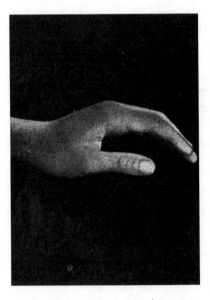 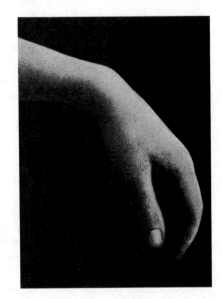

Flinging or tossing the arms from the elbow is the worst possible form of conducting motion. The angle of the arms at the elbow should rarely vary from a norm of ninety degrees.

Following are further exercises designed to strengthen the student's mastery of different metric patterns and his power of concentration.

1. Alternate two measures each of 2/2 and 4/4, keeping ♩ = ♩. Observe carefully that the *quantity* of motion remains approximately the same. If the total conducting motion of a measure were traced with a string, the same length would serve for the 2/2 and the 4/4 patterns. Thus the 4/4 figure, with its greater number of curves, will be composed of smaller individual motions than the 2/2 figure.

Figure 13

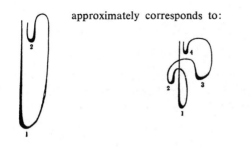

approximately corresponds to:

If this relationship is observed, the student will avoid a (often) dragging tempo for the 4/4 meter. Similar exercises might be applied to 6/8, 9/8, and 12/8 meters. Here the normal pattern (Fig. 1a) should always be alternated with the "cone"-shaped pattern (Fig. 2a). But again, the total quantity of motion must remain the same. The strongly accented "pulled" conducting figure will thus appear larger than the conducting figure in which all beats are marked.

Figure 14

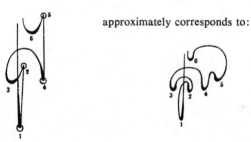

approximately corresponds to:

Changing from one pattern to the other *within* the same measure will at times be required in actual practice.

Figure 15

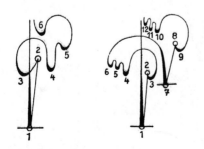

2. The following exercise will prove particularly useful for obtaining the technical facility needed in contemporary music with its frequently changing

meters. Conduct the series of meters given below, always keeping the tempo strictly uniform:

$$\|: \tfrac{2}{2} / \tfrac{3}{4} / \tfrac{3}{2} / \tfrac{4}{4} :\| \text{ or } \|: \tfrac{3}{4} / \tfrac{4}{8} / \tfrac{3}{4} / \tfrac{3}{8} :\| \text{ or } \|: \tfrac{3}{4} / \tfrac{6}{8} / \tfrac{4}{4} / \tfrac{3}{8} / \tfrac{5}{4} / \tfrac{9}{8} :\| \text{ or } \|: \tfrac{4}{4} / \tfrac{3}{2} / \tfrac{4}{4} / \tfrac{6}{8} :\| \text{ or } \|: \tfrac{3}{4} / \tfrac{2}{2} / \tfrac{6}{8} / \tfrac{2}{4} / \tfrac{3}{8} / \tfrac{2}{2} :\|.$$

It is feasible to use the "cone"-shaped pattern for the 6/8 and 3/8 measures in the last two groups: the overall tempo is apt to be too quick to allow for a clear marking of each beat.

Similar sets of changing meters may be devised by teacher and student. It is best to repeat the sequence of two successive measures many times before going on to the next pair. Follow this procedure throughout, so that the entire series becomes absolutely secure. To keep the tempo strictly $\dot{\cdot} = \dot{\cdot}$, have in mind the smallest note value from the very beginning, letting it visibly enter the conducting motions at the appropriate moment. The magnitude of the beat must always remain proportionate to its duration: eighth-beats must be small, quarter-beats, normal size, and half-note beats, large and of flowing motion.

Subdivided Beats

The following section deals with the important problem of dividing the beat through an interpolated motion. Subdivision is needed whenever the regular beat is insufficient to define meter and rhythm. It applies to transitions from one tempo to another, to final retards, and on occasion to entrances between the regular beats. It should be added that it is not advisable in brief changes from a regular to a subdivided 2/2 meter (often found in older music) to alternate 2/2 and 4/4 patterns. The 2/2 pattern should be subdivided instead.

Figure 16

when subdividing a whole measure:

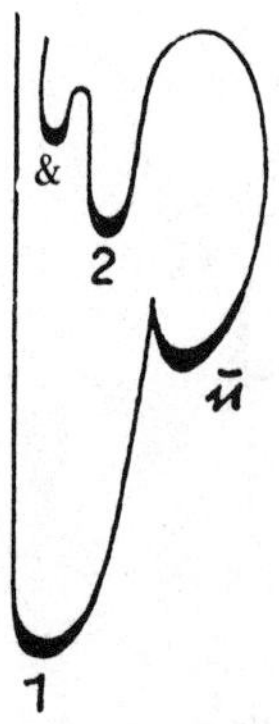

when subdividing a half measure:

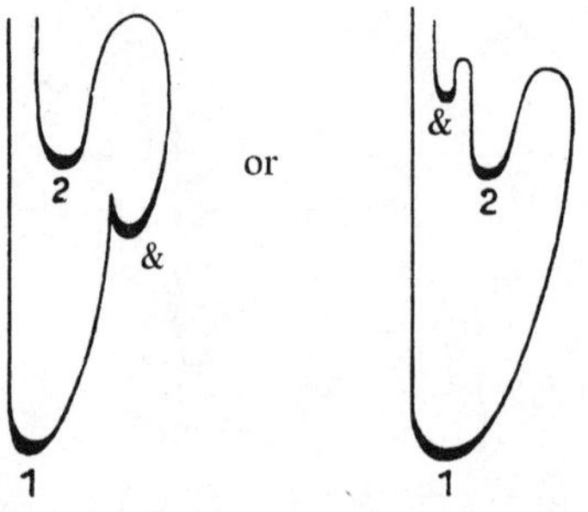

a) "Bouncing" subdivision

A type of subdivision by which special precision can be obtained is in stopping the release of each beat midway. The hand rests at this point, using this level as a springboard. At the point where the beat is to be divided—at the count of "and"—the hand bounces off the imaginary springboard. This bouncing motion must be extremely intense (suggesting a springboard with relatively little elasticity) and turn by force of gravity into the actual "dive." This in turn is followed by the release that follows any regular beat. There is, of course, a great difference between a motion guided by a strong imaginary force and a mere lifting of the arm which would be meaningless as a conducting gesture.

Figure 17

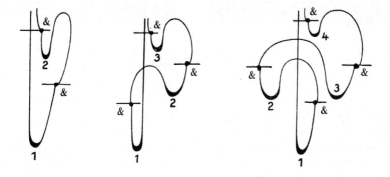

In practicing this motion it will be useful at first to let the palm of one hand serve as the springboard. The other hand, which performs the motion, must remain in a straight line with the arm, without a noticeable bend of the wrist.

b) Subdivision through the wrist

Although the wrist must normally be kept still, a wrist motion may serve at times for a subdivision of the beat; the special motion discussed below should be completely at the conductor's command. Practice this at first in conjunction with an even up and down motion of the arms—using one arm at a time and then both. There should be no stopping between the up and down motion. While the arm moves up, the wrist should point down; at the moment the arm goes down again the wrist must be thrown upward into the position that should be retained during the entire downward motion of the arm (Tables VIc and VId). Since this is a strenuous exercise, the loosening and relaxing motions discussed at the beginning of this chapter should frequently be interspersed.

Table VIc   Table VId

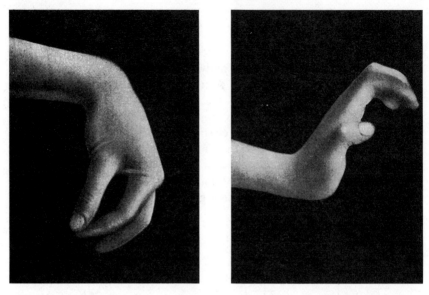

The arm motions merely represent regular beats taken from any metric pattern—their downward push and upward release (cf. Fig. 6). Once this is realized there will be no particular difficulty in integrating the wrist motion into any of the metric patterns. Practice the application of this wrist motion by changing gradually from 2/2 to 8/8 and back, as follows: Begin with a rather spirited 2/2 and, in slowing down to where the count of "1-and-2-and" becomes feasible, start applying the wrist motion on "and." Slowing down further, change to 4/4. Then slow the 4/4 beat down to where this can be subdivided. Then change from the subdivided 4/4 to 8/8 and finally reverse the entire procedure, returning in gradual stages to 2/2.

In practicing a similar change of patterns in triple meter, begin by beating one to a measure, letting the beat of "1" bounce back immediately. Next apply the wrist motion, lowering the wrist at the beat of "1" and adding the beat of "3" with a quick upward fling of the wrist as the arm reaches its highest point. From there proceed to three beats, eventually beating six. The counting pattern would thus be: 1 / 1 / 1 / 1—3 / 1—3 / 1—3 / 1—2—3 / 1—2—3 / 1—2—3 / 1 and 2 and 3 and / 1 and 2 and 3 and / 1 and 2 and 3 and / 1—2—3—4—5—6 / 1—2—3—4—5—6 / 1—2—3—4—5—6 / 1 and 2 and 3 and / 1 and 2 and 3 and / 1 and 2 and 3 and / 1—2—3 / 1—2—3 / 1—2—3 / 1—3 / 1—3 / 1—3 / 1 / 1 / 1.

Practice this with large flowing motions (*legato*) and with quick bouncing motions that are short and precise (*staccato*). Again it is important to intersperse loosening up exercises.

Accents

The conductor should be able to employ at a given point any of the special devices that have been discussed. Such ready use of different types of beat is especially required in stressing accents.

Several kinds of accents must be distinguished. Accents of stress usually coincide with longer note values (Ex. 3). But this is not an inflexible rule: the note value of the note requiring an accent of stress may not be different from its rhythmic context (Ex. 4). Short accents—a rapid pinpointing of

Ex. 3

Now   is   the month   of   may - ing

Ex. 4

O   the plea-sure   of   the   plains

an important note—apply mostly to light vowels (Ex. 5). The accent of

Ex. 5

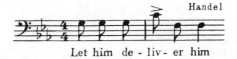

Let him de - liv- er him

stress should be conducted by placing the motion slightly forward—away from the body—possibly opening and turning the hand somewhat, back of the hand down. The best way to practice this is to accent various beats of an unchanging metric pattern that is continued at some length.

Short accents may be indicated by bouncing back from the lowest point of the beat very quickly or—more incisively—by a very rapid dropping and recoiling motion of the wrist precisely on the beat. Extremely light accents may be indicated by a finger motion (Table IVa and b). Extremely heavy accents may be supported by a wrist motion. In this case the wrist should drop down immediately *before* the downbeat, aiming down during the beat (Table VIc); it should bounce up again at the lowest point of the beat (Table VId) and thus lend the downbeat unusual force.

In view of the practice situation in a small class the following series of examples has been so designed that the music can be performed by any combination of voices. (It has been necessary to•reduce or adapt the score in some instances.)

Examples for Entrance and Cut-off

Ex. 6

with God

Hum and check the pitch; then assume the preparatory position.

The preparatory position should convey the utmost concentration (Table VII); the conducting motions should be incisive. Give "two" as the preparatory beat while inhaling; then the entrance on "three" follows. From the outset the conductor should *sing* with the chorus—or at least suggest his direct participation in the performance so that the chorus can "read his lips." An inanimate facial expression and a closed mouth will negate all that the conducting motions are intended to convey. The conducting

Table VII

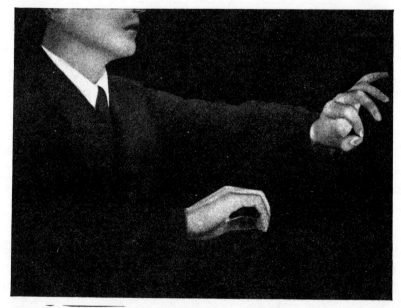

motions on "three" and "four" must be very precise. On "one" of the following measure the motion bounces back to the normal position; from there the arms are slowly and steadily raised to retain the necessary tension for the fermata. For the cut-off bring the arms down and slightly out very rapidly, bounce back to the normal position, and remain so just long enough to do justice to the impact of this *fortissimo* ending. The cut-off and its release must give the effect of *one* motion; there must not be the slightest lingering at the lowest point. This may cause the conducting student considerable difficulty at first and may require a great deal of practice.

Ex. 7

A -   -   - men

This example requires a composed and somewhat cautioning preparatory position (Table 3). The preparatory motion is the beat of "two" given while inhaling calmly. Then beat a gentle and rather slow 2/2 lightly subdivided by the wrist motion (see p. 25). During the fermata gradually raise the arms again. The cut-off occurs by letting the arms fall down and back into place while the final *n* is sounded unhurriedly.

A combination of these two exercises (Exx. 6 and 7) will serve for the practice of a particularly important conducting problem—the problem of concentrating upon different tempos and their connection in *attacca* entrances. After cutting off the fermata of Example 6, remain in what will be the preparatory position for the next entrance. Do not allow the tension to relax until the preparatory beat for Example 7 is given; inhale quietly.

Examples for Different Meters

Common Time

Ex. 8

(Middle part to be omitted or used for additional practice according to the number of available singers.)

Begin this example from the normal preparatory position. The preparatory beat is "three" and the entrance follows on "four." Beat a precise and very lightly bouncing 4/4. The motions of the lower arm must occur without any movement of the wrist. Mark slight accents of stress (see p. 27) on "one" and "three" in measures 4 and 8, on "three" in measure 9, on "one" in measure 10 (that is, do so whenever the word accent requires it). In the last three measures, the accents on the word *no* should be supported by a slight anticipation of the voiced consonant *n*.

Triple Meter

Ex. 9

Begin this example from a rather relaxed preparatory position. The preparatory beat is on "three" and the entrance on "one." The pattern of 3/4—in this case used in a rather gentle and flowing manner—should be subject to slight changes depending upon the expressive quality of various portions of the example. Measures 1 and 2, 4, and 6—9 should be *legato* in character, whereas beats "two" and "three" in measures 3 and 5 should be slightly *marcato*. The suggested crescendos, intended to help sustain the phrase in measures 4—5, 6—7, and 8—9, should be indicated in each case by placing the conducting motions slightly forward.

At this point a conscious leading of different voices should begin, depending upon where the important melodic lines occur. The "conducting part," marked in the score by the dotted line, shows which parts require the conductor's primary attention at a given point.[2] Again: the performance will be alive only if the conductor will sing, or suggest he is singing, what he is conducting. The cut-off in this example should occur on "one" and may be slight (finger motion only, see Table VIII).

Table VIII

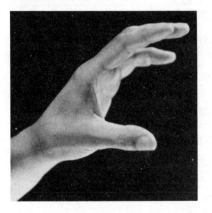

Compound Time

Ex. 10

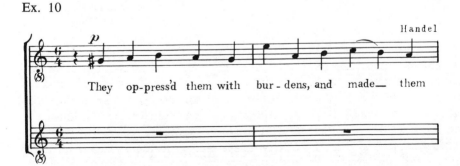

---

[2] This important matter is treated more fully on page 58.

The character of this piece requires a somewhat cautioning preparatory position, but the meter nevertheless requires a precise "one" as the preparatory beat. The 6/4 beat should be calm, with noticeably smaller motions on "two," "three," "five," and "six" than on "one" and "four." At times the beats of "two" and "five" may become so small that the total pattern approaches that of 4/4. This pattern may change to the "cone"-shaped pattern (Figure 2a) in measures 6—8, and a calm 2/2 pattern in measures 10—12. The conducting part will necessarily follow the pattern of entrances but should be marked and consciously observed.

Two-Four Time

Ex. 11

Canon   Beethoven

I pray you, I pray you, sing me the C Ma-jor

scale! Na-na-na-na-na-na-na - na,   na-na-na-na-na-na-na-

na,   na-na-na-na-na-na-na - na,   na-na-na-na-na-na-na - na.

Practice the melody first in unison, then as a round. The preparatory position must suggest complete concentration. A precise beat on "two" serves as the preparatory beat. The entrance occurs between beats and should be aided by a motion of the head or possibly by a small but exact wrist motion. Observe short accents (>) and accents of stress (−).

When sung in parts, the canon will require a repeat of the first entrance for the second and third parts: turn to each new part again on "two." After singing the canon through several times, raise the left arm in preparation for the fermata ending, hold the fermata for all voices, and give the cut-off. (In the Classical round the voices normally end together.) The conductor will find this example especially useful for testing his ability to communicate his directions—that is, to indicate crescendos and decrescendos as well as sudden dynamic changes from *forte* to *piano*. Always "lead" the part that has the text.

Fast Triple Time

Ex. 12

Canon   C. Praetorius

1.   2.   3.   4.

Out of e - ter - ni - ty this day ——— is born, ———

In - to e - ter - ni - ty it will ——— re - turn.

(Text adapted from Thomas Carlyle)

The first of the examples given here should still be conducted with three beats to a measure, but observe that this 3/2 meter should be livelier and more strongly accented than the 3/4 in Example 9.

Practice this example, too, first in unison and then as a round. The preparatory position must suggest complete concentration. The preparatory beat is on "three," the entrance on "one." The second, third, and fourth parts are again cued in by repeating the entrance for the first: turn to each new part precisely on "three." The complete conducting part is quite simply:

Ex. 13

This means that the conductor must change to a new part at every measure. After the canon has been sung through several times, the ending should be indicated for each voice in turn. (In the older canon literature the voices usually finish the canon melody one by one. It is recommended, however, that the first three parts hold their final note until the fourth part has reached the end.) The final note should be ended with a precise cut-off.

Ex. 14

The lively triple beat in early music should usually be executed by using the pattern of a duple meter, whose second beat is placed on the actual count of "three." In the resulting "cone"-shaped figure, "one" is marked quite heavily, "two" is merely suggested (cf. the "cone"-shaped pattern, Fig. 2a), and "three" is indicated by a light beat. To fix the tempo clearly, however, it is recommended that three beats (using very small motions) be given for the first measure; thus one quarter should be given as a preparatory beat. After turning to the "cone"-shaped pattern in the following measures, it is desirable to approach the pattern of one-beat-to-a-measure (especially if

the patterns of ♩♩ and ♩.♩♩ continue at some length in such a piece). In this case the beat of "one" bounces up again immediately; at the same time the wrist must be dropped and sharply brought up again at the highest point of the release to suggest "three" (cf. the discussion of the wrist motion on p. 25). This subdivided beat is much more precise than the beat of one-to-a-measure, but it offers the same fluency of tempo. Only if the tempo is decidedly quicker than that of this example would a bouncing beat of one-to-a-measure be appropriate. At measure 7, however, the conducting pattern should revert to three beats. To gain security in changing from one pattern to another, the following preparatory exercise will prove useful: (1) Conduct three measures of one-beat-to-a-measure; (2) three measures of a divided beat-to-a-measure (wrist motion); (3) three measures of "cone"-shaped triple pattern; (4) three measures of three beats each (small motions); and (5) reverse the entire sequence without interrupting.

Changing Meter

In the performance of Medieval and Renaissance music, the choral conductor must deal with the problem of changing meter on a very large scale. The beat is invariably the central metric unit—its rhythmical value varying according to the particular transcription of the original notation—and this metric unit represents the normal pulse of the music (*tactus*). Because this unit is marked by both the downward and upward beat, the conducting pattern is most often that of 2/2. But this pattern is subject to frequent variation, depending upon the freely changing word accent. Thus the conductor will actually have to alternate between patterns of duple and triple meter.

This necessitates an especially careful preparation of the score—part by part—and of the conducting part. The greater his sensitivity toward the innate rhythm of different voices in a polyphonic texture, the better prepared the conductor will be to deal with the changing meters of modern music. Although the rhythmical complexity is apt to be greater in modern music, its problems as a whole are simplified through the use of a notation by which changing meters are clearly indicated.

The best way to deal with the rhythmical complexities of a choral score will always be the careful preparation of the individual part, and thus the conductor should gain experience in conducting an unaccompanied melody moving in free meter.

Ex. 15

In my des-pair I cry to Thee, Lord God, hear Thou me call - ing.
Lend Thou Thine ear un - to my voice and hear my sup- pli - ca - tion.

If Thou dost mark in - i - qui - ties, heed all our man - y

fra - il - ties, who, Lord, can stand be - fore ___ Thee?

The accent of the text is always the most important factor. Its proper observance will dictate the metric changes, and thus the proper phrasing of both the text and music. The conscious aim of the conducting motions should be toward the last stress of each phrase.

The places where the singers are to take a new breath must be indicated by a slight lifting motion. In conducting a melody with many repeated tones it is important to stress the upward tendency of conducting motions; otherwise the intonation and tone quality will suffer (cf. p. 56).

Polyrhythmic Meter

In giving full attention to the metric patterns of different lines within a polyphonic fabric, the conductor comes to grips with the question of polyrhythmic texture. This is a typical conducting problem in modern music.

To gain sufficient independence in juxtaposing two different meters—this is especially important when the polyrhythmic texture occurs in a slow tempo—the following exercises are recommended:

1. Walk or count in quick triple meter while conducting 2/4 or 4/4.
2. Conduct 3/4 or 6/4 while walking or counting in 2/4.
3. Follow the measure units of a relatively lively 3/4 or 6/4 piece but conduct 2/4 or 4/4; then reverse the procedure: conduct 3/4 or 6/4 for a piece written in a relatively slow 2/4 or 4/4 meter.
4. Sing a melody written in a fairly lively triple meter (for example, *The First Noel*) and beat 2 or 4 for each measure; then sing a melody in a fairly slow duple meter (for example *Frère Jacques*) and beat 3 or 6 for each measure.

Practicing these exercises will help to establish the concept of polyrhythmic texture. When conducting polyrhythmic patterns begin by using the arms alternately: beat 3/4 with the right then 2/4 with the left, then reverse, and finally combine the two. Do the same with 6/4 and 4/4. The beats of the triple pattern should be small and precise, those of the duple pattern quite large and gentle. The more contrast there is in the motions of both arms the easier the combination. Triple meter should always serve as a basis since duple meter can be more easily integrated; its beats actually occur exactly midway between two beats each of the triple pattern. To approach triple meter from the basis of duple meter would be infinitely more difficult. The coinciding beats—"one" in 2/4 and 3/4; "one" and "three" (= "four") in 4/4 and 6/4—should always be strongly emphasized.

Further Study

Once the preceding exercises are mastered, and while working on the following chapters, the student should plan to conduct a number of short examples from the polyphonic literature (madrigals, motets), working at first with the other students as a chorus and eventually with his own group. Invariably the preparation of a conducting part (which may be changed or adapted in the course of the work) should serve as the point of departure. In giving cues the conductor must turn to the section concerned always *exactly one* beat before the entrance to allow enough time for breathing. (This procedure was practiced in the canons given above.) Unless a new entrance commands the conductor's attention he must lead the part that is rhythmically or melodically the most important at the moment; and whenever he is not actually singing this part he must clearly suggest its performance.

To strengthen the conductor's power of concentration it will be useful occasionally to vary the placing of the different sections of the chorus (see also Chapter 8).

Working on different examples from the literature should serve at the same time as a review of the problems discussed in this chapter.

Subconscious Mastery of Technique

Having dealt with all the basic demands of conducting technique in theory and practice, the conductor should not hesitate to begin work with a chorus. At this point, however, we must emphasize that the study material must be so well absorbed that its application is no longer conscious but largely subconscious. To be consciously concerned with conducting motions or patterns while rehearsing or performing a work would be foolish. If the conductor has sufficiently dealt with matters of technique, the right motion will be there at the right moment; it is not the individual motion that matters so much in presenting a work but a clear concept of phrase and continuity. The conductor's concern must move from technical problems to that of interpretation, which is his goal. Many technical obstacles will disappear once the conductor becomes fully involved in the realization that the interpretation of the work is his primary concern and responsibility.

Some Studies in Concentration

In this section a few exercises are given that will prove helpful in preparing the conductor for typically difficult rehearsal situations. They are designed to strengthen his conducting technique and his ability to deal with several rehearsal problems simultaneously.

Various polyphonic scores—ranging from easy to more difficult works and including changes of meter—are to be used in the following manner:

1. The bass part is played on the piano with the left hand, while the conductor is alternately seated and standing. At the same time he sings one of the inner voices and beats time with the right hand, using an even, lightly bouncing beat.

2. The bass part is played in the same manner, while each entrance of the other parts (even those that occur after very short rests) is called out precisely one beat before the voice in question is to come in ("alto"; "tenor," etc.). In addition the conductor beats time with the right hand.

3. The left hand plays the bass part while the right hand beats time and one of the other parts is sung. This is done with *immediate* change from one part to another as they are called out by the instructor.

4. The right hand beats time while the left hand plays any of the parts; again change from part to part as they are called out. The student should do this preferably without looking at the keyboard.

5. Repeat exercises 1 to 4 playing with the right hand and conducting with the left, always using a lightly bouncing beat. Also combine two or three inner parts using either hand and singing one part or calling out the entrances.

6. The student should play a choral score and participate at the same time in a conversation on a totally unrelated topic. (A choral rehearsal will similarly require simultaneous conducting, checking, and explaining.)

7. The student should conduct from a piano-vocal score or a choral-orchestral score while standing at the piano and playing the orchestral basses with the left hand (with a well balanced tone). The orchestral interludes should be played with both hands, but at least one beat before the chorus re-enters, one hand should be conducting again, etc.

Exercises of this kind may seem extremely difficult at first, but they will soon produce a very important result: the conducting technique will have become so well absorbed that the conductor can handle any combination of rehearsal problems—announcing, explaining, giving the pitch, keeping discipline, stressing points of interpretation—while continuing to conduct with ease. It is a matter of attempting what is virtually impossible, to perfect what is possible and desirable.

CHAPTER 3

The Formation of a Chorus

Size of the Chorus

The size of a chorus should depend upon its particular function. For an *a cappella* chorus there should be at least sixteen singers; if there are less it becomes difficult to blend voices into a choral sound, especially if the singers have markedly individual voices. An *a cappella* chorus should at most consist of one hundred voices, provided a light sound and a transparent impression of the contrapuntal texture can be maintained. The ideal size is between thirty and sixty voices. On the other hand, certain works of broader dimensions, such as the *Fest- und Gedenksprüche* by Brahms, can very well be done by a larger chorus.

For choral works with orchestra, the chorus should consist of no more than 150 to 200 voices. The precision of attack is bound to suffer in choruses larger than this; the body of sound becomes fuzzy and thick. We could easily manage with less than we are generally accustomed to today. Bach had only about twenty singers to perform his works. In a small chorus the size of the orchestra must be proportionately reduced.

Of course, for great massed performances—especially outdoors—a chorus of several hundred voices, sometimes even over a thousand, might occasionally be used. But in these cases only broad effects can be achieved; one can scarcely expect true clarity. Such massive performances are only tolerable if the occasion or score calls for such dimensions.

Concerning the ratio or balance of voices within a chorus, it has become customary to have more women's voices than men's, but obviously a well rounded choral sound can be achieved only if the number of men's voices is similar to that of women's voices, especially if there is a good foundation of bass voices. The overtones of bass voices support the sound of the women's and are of great help in producing a well-integrated total sound.

Selection of Voices

In choosing voices for a chorus the main criteria should be the musicality

40

of the chorus member and his attitude toward singing. Consideration of volume and tone quality should be secondary. Needless to say, it is ideal if a singer qualifies in every respect.

A chorus composed exclusively of solo voices—even if the singers are truly musical—is advisable only if they are compatible and if they have been trained through vocal exercises to produce a homogeneous choral tone. An unpleasant effect may be created if several highly individual voices that do not blend in tone color are combined. This can be mitigated, however, by spatial separation or by adding voices of a more neutral tone quality.

A chorus composed exclusively of vocal amateurs can have a dull sound. The best solution is to have some well-trained voices in each section that are then supplemented by "equalizing" voices. Voices with vibrato or a breathy quality must be kept out of the chorus; one such voice can ruin the entire chorus.

Youthful voices are of course always to be preferred. There is nothing worse than an "overaged" chorus with sharp voices and routinized singers who "know everything." It is difficult to set a definite age limit. Many voices seem brittle and old at the age of thirty; others are still fresh and youthful much later. Suitability for a chorus is determined by the quality and attitude of the individual singer.

In choosing voices for each part, Schwickerath recommends the following: [1]

> Requirements for an *a cappella* singer are: a well placed voice, a keen awareness of pitch, a secure sense of rhythm, correct diction, a high degree of general intelligence, seriousness of purpose, patience. A large voice is not necessary; however, the voice must not be sharp, thick or unwieldy. Correct placing of the voice is important above all. Voices which are centered in the throat or palate are not suited for sensitive *a cappella* singing.

> *Soprano:* I warn particularly against "dramatic" soprano voices. Big "lustrous" voices with strong individual character are problematic, in fact, most likely impossible. Graceful, light voices with fine head resonance are the most preferable.

> *Alto:* Real alto voices, indispensable in performing works of the older choral literature with low alto parts and high tenor parts, are even harder to find. Altos with a heavy voice can have a very unpleasant effect upon the choral sound: the all important mastery of a light head register is usually foreign to them.

> *Tenor:* In view of the general dearth of tenors, one should not be too

[1] *Chorübungen,* p. 230.

critical at the audition; however, caution is needed if the choral conductor does not want to make life hard for himself. If all is not well in the audition, it is necessary to determine whether the candidate possesses sufficient insight and intelligence to be able to learn and develop in the right direction.

Bass: One cannot manage without deep bass voices. However, if they are too heavy, they will have trouble singing *mezza voce.* If the quality of voice does not seem right at the outset, the conductor must weigh whether the particular voice in question can be trained.

Obviously all these recommendations are valid only if there is such a large selection of good voices to choose from that the strictest standards can be applied. In all other cases the decision must be dependent upon the interest shown by the candidate. If there is obvious devotion to the cause, it is possible that much can be attained with training, through a preparatory course or an adult education course in ear training and sight singing pursued concurrently with the choral work.

Actually there are fewer truly unmusical people than one ordinarily assumes. Often the "unmusical nature" suggests merely a feeling of inferiority. The same is often true of people who are convinced that their voices are useless because in their youth an irresponsible teacher told them they were unmusical. I have found that voices which were small and timid gradually developed into rich voices with true carrying power.

The range required for the different parts in the chorus is generally as follows:

Ex. 16

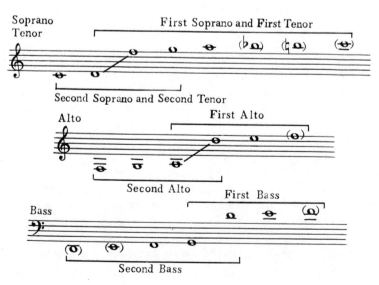

The notes in parentheses are to be considered only in the case of choral works with orchestra or works with many voice parts. The upper and lower limits of these ranges are as a rule to be avoided in two- or three-voiced choral compositions; in a vocal texture of this kind, the conductor will have to assign parts with considerable caution, since he cannot count on the support and the integration of sound due to overtones which arise from a fuller texture.

In the proper distribution of the large number of baritone and mezzo-soprano voices the choral conductor encounters, he should judge the tone quality of each voice; frequently these voices develop upward, especially if they are trained to sing lightly and without strain.

High bass voices can often support the tenor section if their falsetto range is properly trained. Many choral conductors have been successful with this procedure. In fact, quite a few of the voices used in this way have developed into genuine tenors. Similarly, the practice of having some tenors reinforce the alto part (as well as having some altos reinforce the tenor part) will produce very good results, particularly in performing the older choral literature. The conductor will have to exercise due care in choosing suitable voices for this purpose and in seeing that the essential character of each part is not obscured.

Psychological Aspects

Generally speaking, a volunteer chorus is preferable to a paid chorus, unless one is fortunate enough to find singers who sing with complete dedication, regardless of their financial involvement. Otherwise the matter of remuneration is apt to have a demoralizing effect on the *esprit de corps* of a chorus—a psychological factor that should be taken into account.

For that matter, any motive other than dedication in organizing a chorus is bad. The disadvantages arising from forced participation are not outweighed by the addition of a few good and accurate voices. It is preferable by far to have a small chorus made up entirely of enthusiastic singers who are sensitively aware of a common purpose and ideal. Unfortunately, many choruses that began as small and truly unified groups have disintegrated because of a senseless ambition to become big and important.

Thus it is necessary to exercise judgment in selecting new members and not to be softhearted when it becomes necessary to dismiss an old member.

A singer should be let go whenever his voice is no longer suited to the demands of the group or whenever he feels he "knows it all" and does not have to attend all rehearsals. A chorus cannot tolerate exceptions for individuals: any *prima donna* treatment signifies the beginning of the end of a genuinely integrated membership. "The ending is harder to write than a new verse"; nevertheless, to make an end will prove necessary at times—and a choice that will ultimately be wiser and easier on the nerves.

CHAPTER 4

Vocal Training for the Chorus

General Remarks

The subject of this chapter and that of the following on choral diction are interwoven, but they are presented separately to allow a more detailed analysis of each problem. We cannot pursue a detailed course in vocal technique, but we do offer here a survey of practical materials that can be used to train the chorus.

The human voice has different natural "registers" and the singer should attempt to integrate them so as to create the illusion of a single register. This can be done by combining the gentler production and quality of the head tones with the clarity and brightness of the middle register and the richness of the chest register.[1]

Following are some well-tested exercises with directions for their use. They should become routine procedure at every rehearsal to "warm up" the chorus. This will do much for the production and quality of the choral sound, and the singers, whether professional or amateur, will accept them with enthusiasm once positive results are felt (usually within a very short time). "A large percentage of the problems customarily associated with purely musical matters really belong in the realm of vocal technique. It is amazing how quickly difficult melodic and rhythmic passages are mastered if the singer is truly in command of his own voice . . . ."[2]

The conductor must use his judgment in introducing the exercises to a group with which he has not worked before. If the conductor suddenly and without motivation begins the exercises it may do more harm than good, but with enough psychological and pedagogical sensitivity, he will find the right moment. Often the need for exercises will grow out of work on the current repertory, or, ideally, out of the singers' desire of coming to grips with a particular problem.

---

[1] This suggestion is taken from Franziska Martienssen, *Das bewusste Singen* (Leipzig: Kahnt, 1923).

[2] F. Mayerhoff, *Der Chordirigent* (Leipzig: Breitkopf and Härtel, 1922).

Separate make-up sessions might be arranged for new members of the chorus—although it will usually not be difficult for them to reach the technical level of the chorus by participating in the warm-up exercises of the entire group.

Posture of the Singers

To summarize the important points on general posture conducive to a good choral sound, we should emphasize the following:

The entire body should be relaxed. The singer should stand, or "sit as if he were standing"; the shoulders should never be pulled up. In the standing position, one foot may be placed slightly forward, allowing the singer to shift his weight easily.

There should always be the sensation of a slight forward bend of the head suggesting the position, and expression, of a friendly nod. A forced raising of the head (reaching for the *Heldentenor* register) is completely and painfully wrong for a sensitive tone-production.

The lower jaw should "dangle" loose as if entirely directed by gravitational pull.

The mouth should always be rounded, the lips slightly forward, to obtain the greatest possible resonance.

Breathing

The singer should have a sensation of breathing "from the tips of the toes."

Inhale through the nose with the mouth slightly open. (The teeth should be far enough apart to allow space for the tips of two fingers, even when the lips are closed.) The suggestion of a pleasant surprise best conveys the complete relaxation needed to allow the *entire* breathing apparatus to participate in the inhaling process.

The inhaling process is rather rapid, but the exhaling process must be slow and controlled since it results in the formation of sound. Consequently it must be based upon proper "support" from the diaphragm. Good breath control is the essence of good tone.

The choral conductor should become familiar with Leo Kofler's excellent study, *The Art of Breathing* (New York, 1897), which has remained a basic text on breathing technique and tone production.

Humming the Pitch

A fundamental exercise is humming, and in *a cappella* work the conductor will find it useful to have the singers hum their pitches very softly before an entrance in rehearsals—and even before the beginning of a work in performance. This practice allows the singers to sense, and the conductor to check, the proper entrance, and aids both chorus and audience in attaining the desired amount of concentration.

Humming on *ng* will assure the most relaxed sound because it can be done with opened lips. Humming on *m* should be done with the same amount of head resonance (the teeth separated though the lips are closed).

Specific Exercises

To begin, hum some tones on *m* in the middle range of the voice, between e♭ and a♭. The lips are to be so relaxed that they barely touch each other. By cupping the hands behind the ears, each person can check his own sound and resonance. A gentle motion of the head will help to ease and loosen the tone. Do not irritate the vocal chords by roughly clearing the throat. The lower jaw should hang loosely and the tongue be relaxed with its tip touching the inside of the lower teeth. The more relaxed the entire lower portion of the face, the less likely the throat will become dry. Lozenges or dried fruit aid the singer, but not sweets or cold drinks. In the humming exercises the breath support must be maintained with a minimal use of the breath.

Then, with a gradual dropping of the lower jaw, proceed from the *m* hum to a vowel sound between an *a* and *o*. The tip of the tongue remains forward, the lips become rounder and slightly pursed, the head remains loose and the chest somewhat expanded, to maintain proper support.

In a middle range practice all the resonant consonants as well as various vowels, then syllables and words combining important sounds. Whenever possible select material from the text about to be rehearsed.

After these basic exercises, choose some of the following. They should not all be practiced at once, but introduced gradually.

Ex. 17

Beginning on *c* and progressing upward chromatically to *f* or *f♯*, this exercise should be sung quite softly and loosely. Use a calm, swinging 2/2 beat. Each time the final note should be prolonged, at times with a small crescendo followed by a diminuendo that should taper off to a barely audible sound. First hum the exercise, then use normal vowel sounds, changing occasionally to individual notes on *mam-mam-ma* or *nan-nan-na;* color the *m* sound so that it takes on a mixture of *v* and *u*. In exercising, the vowels must be of short duration and the consonants strongly resonant. Remain relaxed throughout, but with good support from the diaphragm. Do not frown.

The loose forward bend of the head must not be changed for the higher tones. Imagine yourself floating, suspended high above the highest notes, and descending gently rather than pulling yourself up to reach them.

The pentatonic series of notes was purposely chosen. It contains none of the difficulties that occur in placing half-steps and thus assures relaxation.

Ex. 18

mi - na mi - na mi - na mi - na mi - na.

Begin softly with the top *c,* then make a slight crescendo, and proceed rapidly with light accents through the sequences of third skips. Shifting from the somewhat covered vowels *i* and *a* to the forward placed resonating consonants *m* and *n* is a valuable aspect of this exercise. Conduct with very light motions, possibly rolling the wrist. Descend a fourth in chromatic steps until the lower *c* is reached as the final note. Remind the chorus of correct posture and breath support.

Ex. 19

nannann *etc.*   na.
(*also* mam-mam . . .)

The third exercise provides practice in placing light accents. It is to be taken upwards a fourth chromatically to *g.* The formation of the consonants is important here and should never be tense. This exercise is to be done rapidly, lightly, and very softly. The vowel sounds must be quite short and the consonants as resonant as possible.

Ex. 20

mam - mam - mam - mamm -   mom - mom - mom - mom -

mum - mum - mum - mu l a - a - a - a   am - mam - ma.

This exercise has proved valuable for various aspects of voice training. It should be done as follows:

1. Relaxed, but with support on a dark *a,* then remaining on a resonant *m* before proceeding to 2.

2. Through the change of vowel the tone is placed farther forward. Imagine singing in an open space. The lips should be pursed slightly. Again, remain on the *m* before proceeding to 3.

3. Imagine the tone coming from *above*. The head resonance must be strong; the support very well maintained.

4. The disjunct tones are to be produced by thrusts from the diaphragm; do not use an *h* sound or a stroke of the glottis.

5. The concluding three notes must be completely relaxed again, as in 1.

Extend this exercise in all its variants to the interval of the fourth, the fifth, etc., up to the tenth.

The following exercise is most effective for cultivating the high register:

Ex. 21

Jun   -   ge, Jun - ge, Jun - ge, Jun - ge, Jun - ge.

(Pronunciation: the "J" as "Yiu"; the "g" not soft, but rather an almost inaudible hard "g" which is merely begun, not completed.)

This exercise should begin softly and reach a crescendo on the first long tone that breaks into the upward fling of the fourth. The latter must be utterly light in tone, like a small ball tossed upward by the surge of a fountain. Then descend rapidly with a series of very light accents, conducting with lightly bouncing motions. Be sure that there is no upward stretching of the head and neck on the top tones.

This exercise should be repeated at ascending half-step intervals; the second tone should be lightly tossed upward and treated effortlessly. If even a single voice in the chorus pushes this note, the exercise should be repeated at that particular pitch. Sometimes do only the first three notes several times. Continue this exercise until an extremely high register is reached without the chorus being aware of the exact pitch—even high *b♭, b* or *c*—which should be placed without effort. This will extend the upper register of the chorus considerably. In the higher pitches start with falsetto, or at least head voice.

The mouth is opened as widely at the beginning as at the end of this exercise, the forward position of the lips does not undergo any change. Diction is only of secondary importance; relaxation is the main point. The lips should always assume the function of the bell of a wind instrument. The coloring of the vowel sounds and the formation of the consonants largely depend on the correct position of the lips. This position need be changed basically only for *m* and *v*.

From time to time it will be useful to sustain a single tone, checking all that has been said about voice production while holding the tone "endlessly" with a minimal use of breath.

Exercise for Choral Coloratura and Non-legato

Ex. 22

This is to be sung repeatedly, using staggered breathing. While consciously checking the relaxed position of the head and the lower jaw, and while maintaining strong breath support, the singer should emit each tone through conscious elastic thrusts from the diaphragm. There must be no audible *h* sound or stroke of the glottis, which must remain open. A small, gentle turning motion of the head accompanying each slur at the beginning of the measure will help prevent stiffness.

Exercise for breath control and endurance:

Ex. 23

Use: mam-mam-mam-mam-m....   ma.

or   mon- nom mon-nom   m....   mo.

etc. until

etc. until

Gradually put several of these patterns together in sequence form, using only one breath:

Ex. 24

etc.

Eventually the complete exercise will be extended for an entire octave and sung in one breath. This will of course require several months' practice.

Without making the chorus specially aware of it, the principles of good vocal training should be carried directly into rehearsal work. Above all, humming the pitch (see p. 45) and singing the rhythm (see p. 64) are devices that will invariably aid in the proper placing and quality of the tone.

CHAPTER 5

Choral Diction

General Considerations

The following discussion, a summary of essential points to be observed in choral diction, can be expressed in one sentence: *Normal speaking and natural speech rhythm should also be applied to singing.*

Obvious as this rule may seem, it is usually violated by grotesque mistakes in pronunciation and accent that would never be made in spoken language. There are many intriguing examples, such as

A quartet, which, singing the ecstatic word, *rapture,* offers in musical but not verbal harmony, "raptyoor," "ratscher," "rahpture," and "rupture." Here we have four simultaneous interpretations of the same word. They have one thing in common: they are all incorrect.[1]

It would be ideal if the conductor could simply ask the chorus to pronounce the words naturally—but our sensitivity has become too dulled. Yet the finest choral sound and rhythm are bound to be lost if the audience cannot understand the words, much less the deeper meaning of the text.

Natural Speech Rhythm

The crucial criterion for a clear understanding of the text is word accent —a constant alternation between heavy and light, long and short. This alternation forms the speech rhythm and governs the meaning of words and the meaning of phrases. (And it is very important for the choral singer to understand and interpret the proper punctuation.)

[1] Madeleine Marshall, *The Singer's Manual of English Diction* (New York: G. Schirmer, 1946), p. 2.

The conductor will repeatedly have to make the chorus aware of speech rhythm, speaking the text himself, and then having the chorus repeat it. Great care and patience are needed when the light syllables are on higher or longer notes than the accented syllables. If handled well, this unusual prosody adds a special charm to the correct diction which should not be destroyed (Ex. 25).

Ex. 25

Occasionally it will be useful to demonstrate the *wrong* mode of diction. The senseless and ridiculous equalizing of stressed and unstressed syllables may do wonders in directing the singers' attention towards natural diction. The most instructive example may be the example of "singers who communicated nothing to their listeners because they ejected the words in the manner of automatons, ma k ing ev e ry syl la ble stand out sep a rate ly." [2]

Without the observance of speech rhythm, all precision in pronouncing consonants and all care in giving the proper color to vowels will be lost. On the other hand, speech rhythm *alone* cannot solve all diction problems. It will be necessary to deal systematically with the diverse functions of vowels and consonants to be able eventually to synthesize all complexities of enunciation in a natural performance of diction.

Translators' Note:

The remaining sections of this chapter, dealing with vowels, consonants, and their combination in various special situations of diction, are so closely linked to specific phenomena of the German language that they are not suited for a direct translation. The reader is referred to the excellent discussion of parallel problems in *The Singer's Manual of English Diction* by Madeleine Marshall. Quotations from this book have been interpolated in the translation of the foregoing text.

Miss Marshall has divided her work into two parts. The first part deals with both voiceless and voiced consonants; the second part deals with both single vowels and their combination as diphthongs.

Vowels and diphthongs are treated in a single section in the work by Kurt Thomas. The most important general advice given in his discussion is that all vowels should be sung with rounded rather than spread lips to allow for a maximum of resonance. (This corresponds to the cardinal advice given in the opening section on vowels in *The Singer's Manual of*

[2] Marshall, *op. cit.*, p. 3.

English Diction—relaxation of lips.) Thomas's section on consonants is divided into a discussion of voiced consonants (*Klinger*) and voiceless consonants (*Nichtklinger*). Great stress in his text is placed upon cultivating the voiced consonants (especially *m, n,* and *l*) as *carrying* the choral sound, in fact, as characterizing its refinement. The voiceless consonants are designated by Thomas as rhythm-giving elements. The importance of all consonants is summarized in his statement that they lend the essentially expressive force to diction; cf. a similar formulation in *The Singer's Manual of English Diction:* "They project the voice. They focus it. They enhance its volume. They supply carrying power. They are as vital to singing an effective *pianissimo* as in creating a stirring *fortissimo.*" [3]

---

[3] Marshall, *op. cit.,* p. 4.

CHAPTER 6

Problems of Intonation

General Reasons for Faulty Intonation

It is often said that flaws of intonation are beyond the conductor's control: intonation is supposed to be subject to weather, temperature, tiredness—that is, the conductor can do no more than take a fatalistic attitude. Obviously this is not so. Although there is some truth in the idea that such things as weather conditions are to be blamed, the truth is that the conductor must be blamed.

There are definite technical reasons for faulty intonation, and the conductor can certainly cope with these more easily than with climate and fatigue. But he must deal with them systematically and make the chorus fully aware of them.

One of the main reasons for bad intonation is tenseness in placing the tone. This problem can be solved by giving the chorus adequate vocal training. (See Chapter 4.) Avoid any suggestion of "pulling" the tone or "pushing" the intonation; ban such words from your vocabulary; they may produce precisely the opposite of the result intended. The only effective means of loosening up the tone production is in "thinking from above." Thinking from a higher register, with a light bend of the head, and the idea of gently rising on tiptoe will be helpful in correcting intonation.

Another reason for intonation problems may be a dark vowel sound. Brightening up this sound will often suddenly improve the intonation. Insufficient breath may also be a cause, which deeper breathing and support may correct. A further reason for intonation problems may be the choice of key. A key that lends emphasis to tones surrounding a change of register (*d-e-f; d-e-f* sharp) may place such a strain upon the voice that the intonation will suffer. If the piece were sung a half-tone higher, the awkward *tessitura* would be avoided and the chorus would stay on pitch. Do not assume that the high register in itself imposes a strain upon the voice and that to transpose down necessarily improves matters. Again the crucial factor is a light, careful placing of the tone without undue tenseness.

54

Specific Intonation Problems

Specific intonation problems will invariably arise from specific problems of voice production. A typical situation is the use of repeated tones. The tone "wears" and will go flat unless it is raised by consciously renewed careful placing. The difference from one repetition of the tone to another may be ever so slight, yet the sum total can amount to a considerable deviation in pitch.

Ex. 26

Fa la la la la la, Fa la la la, Fa la la la *etc.*

This holds true both for the immediate or close repetition of a tone and for the recurrence of the same tone within a larger melodic context.

Ex. 27

I will for spite _ go __ run and slay me, I

will for spite go run __ and __ slay __ me.

Curiously enough, most choral conductors are unaware that this is one of the main causes of bad intonation. Yet it is so easily remedied.

A similar problem is posed by the major third. Keep in mind that as a leading tone the major third must be placed higher than it would sound in the tempered scale. Needless to say, the intonation of the *a cappella* chorus should follow the untempered, not the tempered scale. Thus the same note may have to be treated differently, according to its harmonic context, if the intonation is to remain perfect.

Ex. 28

Further intonation problems are connected with the ascending major second, often not spaced widely enough, and the descending minor second, often spaced too widely. Descending scales are apt to become flat. It will be necessary to suggest some "points of support" to the chorus—normally the fifth, third, and root of the triad contained in a descending scale—and to imagine the pitch of these tones particularly high.

Ex. 29

Ah,   fin   de   la   mia   vi - ta.

Unsuspected intonation difficulties arise from the skips of the fifth and fourth, especially in the bass. A typical progression, such as that in Example 30, poses many problems.

Ex. 30

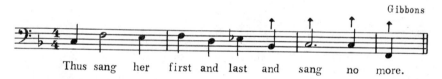

Thus sang   her   first and last   and   sang   no   more.

At times difficulties of diction have an influence upon intonation. Such places must be practiced very softly, "on rhythm" (see p. 64), and the text should not be resumed until the intonation is corrected. Humming the pitch before practicing an entrance (see p. 45) will be of great help in increasing the chorus's sensitivity to intonation.

Pianissimo endings are also apt to become flat. To avoid this, the tension of the performance must be consciously maintained, and there must be enough re-breathing.

Correction of Intonation through Conducting Motions

Even though all intonation problems may have been cleared up during rehearsals, the conductor may lose what has been gained if his conducting motions do not show enough lightness and elasticity. Avoid any suggestion of forcing or driving the tone up. It only leads to strain, undue tension, and thus increases intonation trouble. If in spite of all precautions the pitch is lowered at some point, there is enough opportunity in an *a cappella* work to raise it again—for instance, at passages with repeated tones, or in unison passages. If the pitch should be raised in the excitement of performance, it will suffice to omit the typical lifting motions in conducting or to place the arms somewhat lower until the flaw is corrected. The rise of no more than a quarter-tone will not do any harm; in fact, a somewhat sharp intonation will enhance the sound if there is no undue strain placed upon the voices. On the other hand, a slight lowering of the intonation will result in a weakened, colorless sound and should be avoided under any circumstances.

CHAPTER 7

The Choral Rehearsal

The paramount requirement in a rehearsal is to achieve the greatest result in the shortest time with the least strain to the singers, vocally and generally. At the same time, each rehearsal should be an occasion that rises far above daily chores and provides a valuable experience for every member of the group. The following discussion will deal with specific points that may be of help in achieving these goals.

Preparation of the Conductor

The conductor must be master of every detail and be aware of the inherent difficulties of the scheduled work *before* the first rehearsal.

The best method of learning the work is to study the score so thoroughly that the conductor can clearly imagine its sound. He should then practice the work at the keyboard, singing each part several times, so that he will become fully aware of each melodic line and of the entire polyphonic texture and learn every part almost by memory. This procedure will show without fail where particular attention will be required later.

The conductor should also memorize the "conductor's part." This includes all entrances and all parts that contain significant lines or special problems. In actual conducting, this "part" aids the conductor in concentrating on the voices which should be led and, if need be, supported. The conductor's part, if it is to serve its purpose, runs like a red thread through the fabric of the score and should be memorized as conscientiously as every other detail.

In addition, before the first rehearsal the conductor must have decided how he will divide the scheduled work into sections, so that he may practice them separately. He must also determine which individual parts to combine before he has the entire chorus sing. The sections into which the work is divided for rehearsal must be entities in themselves. They should not be so long that the distribution of tasks will become taxing for some and boring for others, nor should they be so short that restlessness results.

58

The conductor should never begin the first rehearsal until he has made an exact rehearsal plan and determined how many rehearsals will be needed to master the work to be performed. (This will, of course, largely depend upon the ability of his chorus.) It is better to plan too many rehearsals than too few. If the rehearsal schedule is inadequate, a new one must be set up. The conductor should never continue to rehearse without an overall plan in mind.

Part Rehearsals

In undertaking a new and difficult work the most economical plan will be to begin with separate part rehearsals. Although it will be a burden for the conductor if, for example, he begins working on a six-part composition by having rehearsals for each part, a six-fold achievement will result if sections of the chorus do not have to wait around during the earlier rehearsals. Thus, at the beginning, part rehearsals are far more rewarding than full rehearsals.

The often heard objection that it is not possible to assemble the singers on different days is not valid. Here the organizational talent of the conductor and the manner in which he has trained his chorus to work with a sense of responsibility will become apparent. Once the chorus knows how much more is achieved—with less expenditure of time for each singer—by having all parts prepared before the first full rehearsal, the conductor has gained an all-important point.

When necessary, separate rehearsals for women's and men's voices may follow the rehearsals for each part or—in the cases of exceptional disposition of voices—even rehearsals for soprano and bass, tenor and alto, soprano and tenor, alto and bass. The arrangement of working with one section immediately before the full rehearsal and with another section immediately after the rehearsal (in preparation for the next rehearsal) is useful. In each of these part rehearsals those places are rehearsed in which the particular combination can produce the best results for the learning process.

Special combinations of parts that might be rehearsed, even in full rehearsals, are as follows: in homophonic music a combination of the outer parts (the "framework") or of the inner parts is recommended; also the lower voices without the soprano, since small irregularities are often concealed because of the preponderance of the soprano timbre. In polyphonic music it is best to combine the parts that are thematically related, such as canonic voices, voices that show a parallel rhythmic structure, theme and countersubject in a double fugue, etc. Where entrances are difficult rhythmically or harmonically, the entering part should be rehearsed with that voice which is most closely related to it, and by which it can best orient itself.

Thus the combination of voices should be chosen either for simplification —to gain a measure of assurance—or for complexity—to gain a measure of security even beyond that which may seem to be actually needed.

Punctuality

And now the first full rehearsal. Punctuality is an important consideration. If the conductor does not invariably start his rehearsal on time he
can scarcely expect his singers to be on time. Chorus members who do
not attend punctually and regularly, in spite of the example set by the
conductor and in spite of his admonitions (which should be addressed to
each person individually), should be excluded from further participation.
It is better to have a small chorus of reliable members than a large chorus
whose work and morale are undermined by the tardiness of a minority.

Discussion of the Work

Should the conductor first describe and play the music for the chorus?
I think every superfluous word should be avoided; the playing or reading
of a work means an unnecessary loss of time. However, this depends on
the work involved; in principle the chorus should become accustomed to
working first. Later, perhaps, this may be assisted by short explanations to
discover the subtleties of the work gradually. In this way the chorus will
doubtless derive greater pleasure and understanding. Concentrating on
problems of rhythm, tone, and diction separately and at different times (to
be discussed below) will offer variety rather than fatigue and, above all,
insure a true grasp of the work's technical problems.

Training Toward Individual Responsibility

The energy of the conductor should be directed toward accustoming the
chorus to work with undivided attention and toward preventing any lack of
concentration. Members of the chorus must not talk or let their attention
wander during the rehearsal, even when they are not singing. If any dis-
turbance should arise, the best way to deal with it is to wait until everyone
is quiet—eventually even the least sensitive member will realize what is
expected of him.

Essentially, the conductor must keep interest in his work alive, which is
possible only if he himself approaches his task with thorough mastery and
a competely serious attitude. Seriousness of purpose does not preclude
cheerfulness or a sense of humor. A joke at the crucial moment can mean
a release from tension and bring about a complete change in the situation.

Every minute of the rehearsal must be stimulating for each member of
the chorus. The conductor should always work with full concentration and
without unnecessary words; but short, *pointed* remarks which are of concern to everyone should be made often. The more precise the conductor,
the greater the attention he will command.

Everyone, including professional singers, must feel that they are learning
something, whether it be in the realm of voice production, diction or
general musicianship. No sloppiness should be allowed to pass unchecked;

rhythmic exactness must be achieved and particular attention should be paid to giving each note its correct value.

It is a mistake for the chorus to try to attain its objective in a hurry. The more securely the material is mastered, the more it will be enjoyed and understood. Do not undertake too much. Fewer performances and shorter programs perfectly presented will strengthen the morale of the chorus and the response of the audience.

If a rehearsal break is desired it should only be to provide some fresh air—the time should be used for announcements and discussion of matters pertaining to the chorus as a whole. If possible, discourage the chorus from breaking up into small conversational groups, for such distraction disrupts the work and results in additional loss of time when the rehearsal is resumed.

Rehearsing Without a Piano

As a basic condition, the rehearsal should progress in absolute quiet. The ideal situation is to work without a piano in *a cappella* music, if for no other reason than that the unaccompanied chorus should sing with pure intonation which deviates from the tempered tuning of the instrument. The practice of banging the notes on the piano for each part, often adopted for the convenience of the conductor, must be completely eliminated. It is a mistake to assume that results can be attained more quickly in this way.

The aim should be to use *vocal* demonstration where necessary—the voice should be the point of departure, and every sound foreign to the voice should be avoided. The sound of voice and piano in unison can drive the discerning musician to despair.

If the chorus members are not accustomed to working without an instrument, they will nevertheless realize the advantage of *a cappella* rehearsing within a short time, as the apparent feeling of security that the piano may give vanishes when it is no longer used. Then the work has to start all over again. Why not take a direct—and musicianly approach?

On the other hand, if the work is written with instrumental accompaniment, it will save time to use the piano to give the starting tones and indicate the instrumental bass line or the harmonies to which the chorus must become accustomed. In this case it is also necessary to use the piano so that the chorus can become used to the tempered tuning. In fact, a chorus that is used to *a cappella* work can have such a decided "independence" that it will find it difficult to sing with an instrumental ensemble. Conversely, a chorus accustomed to instrumental accompaniment will find that *a cappella* singing presents many problems. In any case, senseless pounding of the voice parts on the piano is to be avoided.

Placement of the Chorus and Rehearsal Procedure

The arrangement of the chorus in a semicircle with the conductor standing in the center is recommended above all others. This will make it possible for the conductor to be seen and heard by everyone and for the members of the chorus to hear each other.

I think a conductor should not be seated during a rehearsal—except when at the piano to play the orchestral bass. It is best for him to stand, sing, and conduct even during the part rehearsals, to accustom the chorus from the very beginning to his manner of direction and to compel them to respond. Among other things this method offers the advantage that the conductor will naturally find the most suitable technical means for conducting a particular work; he will practice the entrances and difficult spots and thus he will continually develop his conducting technique.

So far as seating the chorus is concerned, a frequent change of standing up and sitting down is tiring and creates a lack of concentration. Having experimented with the problem, I have found that the entire chorus should be seated while rehearsing separate parts and working on details of individual lines and voice combinations. As soon as one section of the work is ready to be sung by the entire chorus, the chorus should stand. If it sits while singing, special attention must be paid to posture—the body from the hips up should be free and should assume the same position as in standing. Sitting with crossed legs or in a slouched position should not be allowed—the only accepted sitting posture is one that suggests the motion of getting up. Obviously one can sing better standing than sitting. But just as the whole chorus cannot be left standing during the entire reheasal, so it is not feasible to have each section get up whenever individual part work is involved.

Counting aloud by the conductor during the singing is out of place; on the other hand, while the chorus has not yet mastered the notes, underline each preparatory beat by clearly pronouncing the particular count. This practice will frequently save time. If the chorus is not yet sufficiently secure to be able to follow the conductor's motions, a sharp light tapping (using a pencil—never stamping the feet) is permissible in places that are rhythmically complicated.

Occasionally sounding a note on the piano to verify or control the pitch can take place without interruption of conducting.

Educating the Chorus Toward Attentive Participation

Any excessively loud word spoken by the conductor is bad, for it is usually taken as an indication of insecurity. It must become a matter of course for all members of the choir to follow each word and thought of the director with undivided attention, and to be so absorbed in the progress of the rehearsal that they can tell in advance what the next step will be.

Members that are not singing at a given time should check the parts which are being rehearsed. (It is a great help to use vocal scores.) In order to achieve attention the conductor must say nothing that is unrelated to the subject, and any criticism must always be pertinent, touching, if possible, on matters of interest to everyone.

Often, while one section is rehearsing, it is advisable to have the others sing their parts very softly on one syllable; thus the chorus will gradually perfect the complete sound.

The conductor should never have a passage repeated without giving a short but valid reason. The chorus should be aware of everything and never work without understanding. It will thus grow continually in independence and maturity.

The more aware a chorus is of its basic mistakes, the more quickly will it be able to avoid them as a matter of principle. Avoiding basic mistakes and tracing their causes will also give each singer a feeling of responsibility, of serving the common task with the same seriousness as the conductor, and of contributing towards a genuine achievement.

Finally, the abuse of "section leaders" (the situation whereby one or several singers take the initiative and others follow) will disappear in such work and a group of equally responsible and dedicated people will form the chorus.

Editions that contain more than the notes and markings written by the composer himself are in essence an insult to the choral conductor (unfortunately at times still justified). Completely out of the question, of course, are editions in which the editor believes he must improve upon the composer—such as the editions of works by Schütz in which five parts have been augmented to six. If you use such editions eliminate everything superfluous. But why not use editions which are true to the original and are generally available?

"Authority" of the Conductor

It is a foregone conclusion that nothing the conductor does is directed toward selfish ends or personal ambitions: everything is done through common devotion to the music. The conductor has no higher sense of himself than of each of his singers and he, as a member of the group, acts with an authority granted him only by virtue of his experience.

Each member of the chorus must realize that his function is as necessary as that of the conductor's. Then the situation will not arise in which certain members feel they are being demoted if, for example, they should be asked to sing second soprano instead of first (or similar imagined hardships).

Authority cannot be won by aggressive compulsion. Where an inner desire to cooperate does not exist, an intense concentration on the task of the chorus is not possible. The human voice is the most sensitive of all instruments and the chorus the most expressive of performance media. If its expression is impaired by insensitive regimentation, a deep impression upon the audience will never be achieved.

Lengthy speeches should rarely be addressed to the chorus. They hardly ever achieve the desired result owing to a tendency that cannot be overlooked: each member will "pass the buck" to the next. This is also true of an orchestra. The conductor must phrase his corrections in short precise terms confined to the most pertinent points; he should call these out preferably *while* the chorus sings. If the singing is interrupted the conductor must not let a silence occur or a debate start. When a section is to be repeated, the place where the chorus is to resume should be stated immediately after the chorus stops. The proper *pacing of the rehearsal* should always be maintained, and the conductor himself must represent this pace by his every word and motion. An awareness of pace can even show itself in turning from one section of the chorus to another—even in the manner of turning pages. However, a studied cultivation of rhythmic sensitivity can easily lead to exaggeration.

The first law remains—that the conductor rehearse with the utmost concentration and a minimum loss of time, and that he work always with deliberation and without nervousness. Useless aggressiveness will cause opposition in his group. A feeling of hurry should never arise in the chorus; the feeling of having enough time, as well as a calm working atmosphere, must always be imparted and maintained.

The realization of this ideal will be aided by a manner of rehearsing that stresses variety and remains alive, and by an understanding of psychological factors. Variety is especially important in the giving of explanations because many things must be repeated without appearing to become threadbare. In studying a work, the practice of not always starting at the beginning has proved eminently valuable; otherwise it often happens that the last part of a piece receives less attention than the beginning. In one of the rehearsals immediately before the performance it is recommended that the final section of the work be rehearsed first, then an earlier section, moving gradually forward so that the opening is rehearsed last. This will mean a fresher state of preparation for singing the entire work in continuity than to begin all over each time—resulting in a relaxing of alertness—and having to return to the beginning once more to sing the entire work.

It is proper to make the chorus fully aware of the difficulties of a troublesome passage. Indeed all problems for the chorus should be discussed frankly. In this way the chorus will understand that a difficult passage must be rehearsed until it has become completely secure and no "anxiety spots" remain. On the other hand the chorus should not be burdened with technical discussions of interest only to the conductor himself. To act, to set an example will be the quickest method for achieving the desired results. In due time the conductor can initiate his chorus into more and more technical details which the chorus will then fully appreciate.

The frequently observed tendency of the beginning conductor to display all of his knowledge and ability to a chorus will not lead anywhere. The goal must be a gradual but ever-growing intensification of accomplishment.

In the following are given some suggestions to help enliven and simplify the rehearsal situation.

Practicing the Rhythm

In a section of a work that presents unusual problems of rhythm or tone production, it is advisable to approach the rhythm or the tone separately from the diction. The section in question should be sung without the text, concentrating on the rhythm and using only the syllables *nan-nan-na* or *mam-mam-ma.* It is best not to use either pattern too often, because constant repetition of the same consonant will lead to tenseness.

The consonants *m* and *n* are the best for placing the tone forward and for helping to achieve pure intonation and clear rhythm. The *n* or *m* must not be formed rigidly, but as relaxed as possible: one should have the feeling that the lower jaw would fall off if it were not held on by the surrounding skin.

In practicing "on rhythm," the vowel should be sustained on the longer notes; but for shorter note values the *n* or *m* should be sounded immediately and used as a hum. (Note that the *m*'s and *n*'s thus receive more prominence than the *a.*)

Ex. 31

As soon as the chorus is used to this device, all rhythmical problems can be solved in a relatively short time. There is the added advantage of better mastery of intonation since the consonants *n* and *m* are a decided help in the voice production; in fact, through such practice, voice production will be unconsciously but steadily enhanced. The more softly this technique is applied, allowing only very light accents, the more effective it will be.

In general, the softer the practicing, the more the rhythm is absorbed by each singer. This combination of assurance and lightness of tone production is the most important consideration of all choral singing.

No good can be achieved by rehearsing with vocal exertion. When the rehearsal is over there should be no tiredness whatsoever. On the contrary, a rehearsal, no matter how lengthy and strenuous, can be truly enlivening and refreshing for each singer provided it is correctly conducted.

Loudness is easily achieved, but often it is merely the result of an inner uncertainty. A *forte* will become effective only when the general level of dynamics takes a *piano* as its basis. This is obvious, but how rarely does one hear a chorus that sings with a fine tone and whose *forte* has carrying power.

Passages that present particularly difficult rhythmic problems should be supported either by tapping each beat with a light bouncing touch of a pencil on wood by the conductor or by a short hissing sound on each beat (which will also result in a softer tone). To mark special accents such as syncopations, lightly clap the fingertips of one hand on the ball of the other. Such support of the beat should be used with discretion until the singers are so secure that they can follow the conducting motions with absolute precision.

Practicing the Text

When the music itself is secure in rhythm and tone, it is necessary to give equally concentrated attention to the words. Sometimes it is helpful to speak the text in a simple, natural way, and then have the entire chorus repeat it. This may encounter some resistance at first; but much can be gained from it once the chorus has been convinced of its effectiveness. It is particularly useful in strophic forms (where sometimes only the first verse is carefully rehearsed, with the result that unexpectedly embarrassing surprises occur in later verses).

When working on consonants, it will be helpful to have the entire chorus whisper the text. It is also recommended that sections of the text that have a common rhythm be sung by everyone on just one tone. This will produce effective results for the formation of liquescent consonants as well as for the correct stress of the words.

The value of choral whispering will gradually be realized as the results of such practice become apparent. It is of basic importance that the conductor speak—or whisper—the text unaffectedly for the chorus with perfect clarity, and with correct stress of the words and tempo. He should also support the choral recitation or whispering with gestures that underline the speech rhythm. These gestures need be no more than very light and bouncing beats that mark the chief accent of each part of the phrase. That such accents do not occur with regularity will at first cause some difficulty. But the important point is that between two accents the conducting motion must continue to suggest a constantly flowing rhythm of the text. As the conductor speaks or whispers the text with the chorus, he should observe the proper breathing points, and he should mark them with a slight upward motion. Once the chorus has overcome its first hesitancy and has realized with what clarity and force the words can be projected through whispering, a great step has been taken toward interpretation. (Naturally the suggestion of each vowel and consonant must be so clear that it can be read from the singers' lips, and the same cannot be recommended strongly enough for the conductor.)

Particular Problems of Rhythm

A particular source of difficulty for almost every chorus is the occurrence of triplets within regular rhythmic progressions in duple meter.

Ex. 32 Brahms

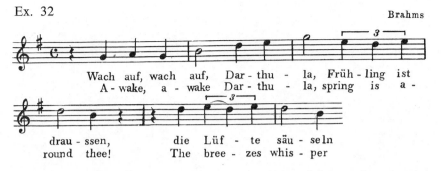

Wach auf, wach auf, Dar - thu - la, Früh - ling ist
A - wake, a - wake Dar - thu - la, spring is a -

drau - ssen, die Lüf - te säu - seln
round thee! The bree - zes whis - per

The usual mistake is to take the first part of the triplet too fast, causing the last note to be lengthened; for instance,

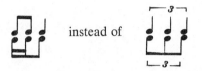

instead of

The conductor can devise special exercises to eliminate this mistake just as he may eliminate many other problems by the use of special exercises dealing with the principles of tone production, diction, or rhythm. This is preferable to repeating the entire passage from the beginning when mistakes occur. In fact, a chorus will sing such exercises with enthusiasm if they are properly presented and if each singer has the feeling he is learning something specific.

Another rhythmical mistake that commonly occurs is that the sixteenth notes are sung too quickly and unprecisely in such passages as

Ex. 33

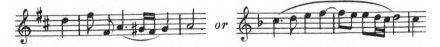

or

The only remedy is to practice the rhythm in the manner described in the previous section.

Occasionally such rhythmically difficult passages can be practiced by taking the tempo twice as slowly—a device that can of course also be applied to problems of intonation or tone production. But it is not recommended to use a broadened tempo too frequently. Some choral conductors make a habit of practicing all difficult passages in a slow tempo, but they fail to realize that the melodic texture (*melos*) is thereby fundamentally altered and that to change later to another tempo means in effect a loss of time.

With some rhythmical problems it is necessary to practice certain clarifying adaptations. The choral conductor can never be inventive enough in this respect. For example,

Ex. 34

zum Bie-nen - kor -   - be ka -   - me
the bees sweet hon -   - ey would____ try

should be sung first "on rhythm," as follows:

Ex. 35

nannann *etc.*

If difficulties persist, an accent or a stress on the second part of the tied note should be used:

Ex. 36

nannann *etc.*

If the passage still does not sound precise, the tie should be temporarily ignored and the repeated tones emphasized:

Ex. 37

nannann *etc.*

Then the procedure should be gradually reversed in order to arrive at the correct performance of the original form of the passage.

Use of Enharmonic Changes

I should like to warn choral conductors of the mistake of changing a difficult interval enharmonically to a relatively simple one. At first this might seem to facilitate reading, but it will actually result in a sensitive intonation problem. Since the original tone is obviously quite different from the substituted tone, the melodic connection with what follows may become quite impossible. The best practice procedure in such a case is to outline harmonically important points. For instance, in Ex. 38, the logical course would be as outlined by the versions numbered 2, 3, 4, and 5. Practicing the passage in this manner will render the intonation correct; whereas practicing the passage in the form of version 6 will inevitably cause the final note *e* to be out of tune.

Ex. 38

Practicing in Unison

Difficult passages occurring at various places in different voices can often be practiced jointly, for example, by having the alto part sung by the entire chorus in unison. If a work is based on a cantus firmus, all voices should first practice the cantus firmus in this manner. This will lead to a fuller understanding of the texture of the work. In movements where the text is set in a similar way for each voice it is economical and advisable for everyone to practice it together rather than part by part; in this way valuable time can be gained to work on matters of interpretation.

Other aspects of unison performance, such as the forming of a gradual crescendo or diminuendo, can be practiced jointly by the entire chorus. Special attention must be paid to the diminuendo. It is difficult to achieve a gradual lowering of dynamics; usually the change will be too sudden. It is useful to practice at first a "terraced" increase and decrease of dynamics, and then a more gradual transition. The conductor should always

Ex. 39

remind the chorus that the start of the crescendo must not be on too high a dynamic level, whereas the beginning of the diminuendo does represent a high point in the dynamic range. Also it may be necessary to warn the chorus of the habit of associating *pp* with a slow tempo, *ff* with a fast tempo, crescendo with accelerando, and diminuendo with ritardando. They are not synonymous!

Giving Precise Directions

The specific manner in which the choral conductor gives his directions should be carefully considered—for example, in announcing an entrance somewhere in the middle of a piece. There is obviously no difficulty if measure numbers are printed in the music. But if the measures are not numbered, and if one wishes to begin, say, eighteen measures before the end, it is impractical to count the measures silently and then announce: "We begin eighteen measures before the end of the piece!", so that a general counting effort gets underway. The direction should rather be phrased: "Counting back from the end of the piece; 1, 2, 3, 4 . . . 18 measures . . ." In this way conductor and chorus count together and avoid loss of valuable rehearsal time.

It goes without saying that the conductor must be familiar with the condition of the parts or scores being used; he must know whether the copies have measure numbers or letters, and whether these agree with those in his own score. If not, adjustments must be made before the first rehearsal. (The conductor must be sure not to refer to a page or staff of the full score unless the singers are also using the full score.)

It is also important not to forget to give the pitch again before a particular place is to be rehearsed. It saves time to give the pitch immediately after announcing the place at which to begin. Both might be done simultaneously by singing the word in the text on its correct note.

Another way to save time is to announce a new entrance twice—that is, to confirm it in a slightly different wording. This might appear at first unnecessary. But even in the best intentioned and best trained chorus singers often rely on each other and fail to take in everything at the moment. For example, if the conductor wishes to repeat a passage "on rhythm," he should first announce this; then, just before the entrance, call out again "on *nan-nan-na*" or "without text," or actually sing the first notes on *"nan-nan-na,"* thus giving the pitch at the same time. Only then can he be relatively sure that *all* members of the chorus will follow the given direction. If only one announcement is made there is always the danger that some members will sing the text and create restlessness and uncertainty, so that it may be necessary to stop and begin again.

In general it is recommended to use a number of short, precise expressions which are understood by the chorus, and which will be effective in various situations. For example: "Lightly!"—"Repeated notes higher!"—"Accents!"—"Drop secondary syllables!"—"Gentle on the high notes!"—"Hum the pitch, please!"—"Tip of the tongue forward!"—"Open mouths!"—"Support!"—"Rhythm only!"—"Think from the top note!"—etc. Such directions will be most helpful when called out with precision and emphasis, yet in a friendly tone and with no trace of impatience. Repeat troublesome spots a number of times without pause. At the moment the passage is finished, give the entrance again after the necessary direction—"once again" or "and again"—until it goes perfectly. Introductions, such as "Would you be so kind as to . . . ," do not appeal to an intelligent chorus and take up valuable time.

Breathing

There are three types of choral breathing:

A deep breath, used at the end of a phrase, where usually a rest in the music will coincide with a punctuation mark in the text:

Ex. 40

A quick, short supporting breath, in which the singers must maintain their breath support. This also applies to the end of a phrase in those places which do not allow sufficient time for a deep breath (see the following example). In such a case special attention must be given not to let the tone be snapped off, but rather lifted gently, an effect which can be encouraged by a light though precisely timed conducting motion.

Ex. 41

Staggered breathing, which is possible only in a chorus and to be used where a long melodic phrase cannot be taken in one breath yet should not be broken at any place.

Ex. 42

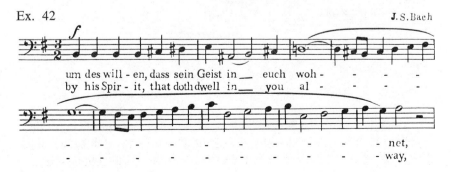

In this case the singers breathe quietly at different times and places, so that the line as a whole remains unbroken. As a rule when there are more than five singers to a part, no noticeable break will occur through this type of breathing. If there are fewer singers to a part, the places where each will breathe must be predetermined—either by the singers or in consultation with the conductor. Above all, this breathing must be done quietly, and the resumption of the part by each singer must take place cautiously and inconspicuously.

Staggered breathing is also to be applied in the case of notes of excessive length, and in performing coloratura passages (discussed in the following section).

Choral Coloratura

Extended coloratura passages need special practice. In the following examples (taken from Bach's Motet No. 3, *Jesu meine Freude*) it would be very disturbing if there were a break at the places marked ↓ , and especially at the places marked ⤳ :

Ex. 43

I have told my choruses: "You may breathe at practically any spot, and the sooner the better; even omit notes to take a breath. But it is taboo to breathe after a dotted note or after a tied note." It is at these places that the highest tension of the melodic line occurs and a caesura must be avoided.

Since coloratura passages of this kind are instrumental rather than vocal in concept, they should not be sung entirely legato but gently detached. However, the separation must not become conspicuous. Each note must be produced with open larynx and elastic diaphragm. The following example illustrates the way to perform such a melodic line: each note marked with a dot is to be slightly marked—not hacked.

Ex. 44

In passages such as those from the Bach motet (Ex. 43), a non-legato of purely even notes is not sufficient to keep the line and motion alive. It is necessary to phrase the passage in the manner of an articulation used for stringed instruments: the first two notes of each group should be joined, and the others separated as described. (This articulation is indicated with slurs in the example given above.) All tied notes must receive a slight increase in intensity. The phrase as a whole must never lose its feeling of progression, and must increase in tension toward its logical destination, that is, the point where the text is resumed.

Even in passages in which two notes are set to a syllable—typical of eighteenth and nineteenth century choral music—each note should be made clear.

Ex. 45

Everything said so far applies only to choral coloratura passages of an essentially instrumental nature (found occasionally in Schütz's works and typical of much of the music of Bach's era). A melodic line conceived in a truly vocal rather than an instrumental style must have all melismas sung legato.

Ex. 46

The appropriate technique applicable to coloratura passages in contemporary choral music must be determined in each case by the character of the particular work.

The articulation of the text in a coloratura passage does not differ in essence from the articulation in passages where each new syllable coincides with a new note. The important syllables must be given the emphasis needed to clarify the meaning of the words. Especially in a somewhat declamatory style of choral writing, groups of notes which are attached, so to speak, after an accented syllable should be taken very lightly, almost like an echo, so that the quality of the choral tone will always be light, never heavy.

Ex. 47

The articulation of the text in a coloratura passage does not differ in

Gaining Security

After a choral piece has been completely prepared, I often have it sung through again "on rhythm," conducting with smaller and smaller motions until the chorus is almost entirely on its own. This helps in giving the chorus the assurance that the piece is secure (but only if the chorus succeeds in singing with utmost precision and with an "inward" rhythm, softly, and without any "anxiety crescendos").

This can never be achieved, however, if the choral conductor simply lets the chorus take over. Obviously, he must observe the chorus with utmost concentration, keeping a strict eye on every entrance and difficult passage, and leading suggestively though practically omitting visible conducting gestures.

The Dress Rehearsal

Since the dress rehearsal is concerned not only with musical problems but also with physical arrangements and the acoustical properties of the hall, it must be held in the same place as the performance and must have the most careful preparation. Every detail pertaining to the placement of the chorus should be attended to before the chorus appears.

There must be sufficient room on the stage for the performers and a podium for the conductor. Risers for the chorus are urgently recommended. The lighting must be examined and tested. It is even important to check on the lighting in the auditorium itself, for the singers might have difficulty in seeing the conductor if a large light fixture right behind him should shine in their eyes. Above all, orchestra players are sensitive about insufficient or poorly placed lighting.

The conductor must acquaint himself with the acoustics of the hall by hearing the chorus from various places during the dress rehearsal. This is important for a final decision of the proper tempo and other special aspects of interpretation. When the conductor leaves the podium, a well trained chorus will continue singing without him; however, if necessary, a substitute may take over.

In halls that are too "alive" with strong reverberation, it is necessary to use broader tempos and longer pauses so that the sound can unfold, and it becomes doubly necessary to use precise diction and to place the proper stress on the important syllables. Halls with "dry" acoustics, causing the sound to die out, sometimes very awkwardly, require more spirited tempos and special attention to the choral legato sound produced by the liquescent consonants.

It is most important that the chorus have a clear impression of the total sound. If necessary, it should be placed in a formation actually approaching a semicircle, with the voices singing toward each other.

In conclusion, a word about the common superstition that to assure a good performance the dress rehearsal must be poor. This may be partially valid insofar as it applies to an inadequate emotional interpretation. On the other hand, lack of precision, wavering tempos, flatting and poor diction indicate insufficient preparation and an unsatisfactory disposition of rehearsal time. If the choral conductor, duly aware of his responsibility, has not undertaken too much from the outset, the dress rehearsal should be perfect—at least in matters of choral technique—so that the performance itself will not turn into a *tour de force,* but rather will be an experience of thorough mastery, deep insight, and true identification with the emotional content of the work.

Addendum

Finally, a few points concerning the performance. On the question of conducting from memory, it goes without saying that the choral conductor should have fairly well memorized the work he is about to conduct. However, he should not make an issue of it by conducting without a score and making a virtuoso performance of something that should be merely a matter of course.

In giving the pitch for *a cappella* works one should not use the piano: its purely instrumental tone quality acts like a foreign substance. It is best for the conductor himself to give the pitch softly for each part, in the range natural to his own voice. Or he should have a member of the chorus give it. After the singers have clearly grasped their tones, they should hum them lightly thus reassuring the conductor and themselves of the certainty of the opening sound. The conductor should help this procedure by careful checking and by supporting gestures. It is better to hum the pitch several times than to be led by a false sense of pride into an inaccurate opening sound; if the humming is done properly it never has a disturbing effect, in fact it will not be perceptible to the audience. (Is there anything more embarrassing for everyone present than having to stop and start over again—a situation that at times arises even with experienced choruses?)

The conductor must not allow the slightest indication of nervousness to appear in the performance or in the rehearsals. Such nervousness is usually only the expression of a guilty conscience because the conductor is insufficiently prepared. But if a nervous state should arise, self-discipline should prevent its being noticed. Under no circumstances should the conductor display any impatience, even when things do not go as well as they should. In the last analysis, he must assume responsibility for everything that is below par; such displays are merely expressions of self-annoyance and do not contribute in the slightest to an improvement of the situation. How can the chorus remain above such matters and perform well if its conductor does not furnish an example? This also holds true in dealing with the soloist.

Obviously the conductor must always lead and interpret in the performance, but he must never become a tyrant. It is preferable on occasion to yield slightly and follow the tempo of the chorus rather than to force it ahead relentlessly. If something does not go well, the conductor must take hold and help. Any excitement in such a situation might cause additional mistakes which could well be avoided. Whether a lack in performance can be traced to insufficient rehearsing, poor training of the chorus, or a lack of composure on the part of the conductor, he himself must always take the blame. The basic attitude towards his work should be: "There are no poor choruses, only ineffectual choral conductors!"

CHAPTER 8

Seating and Standing Arrangements

A Cappella Chorus

Following are the usual arrangements for placing the sections of an *a cappella* mixed chorus; they can always be used when the chorus is on risers or when the room is in tiers. (For a four-part men's chorus, substitute the first tenor for the soprano, the second tenor for the alto, the first bass for the tenor, and the second bass for the bass of a mixed chorus; for a four-part women's chorus, substitute the first soprano for the soprano, the second soprano for the alto, the first alto for the tenor, and the second alto for the bass of a mixed chorus.)

Diagram 1: Four-voice arrangement:

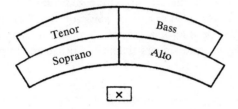

Diagram 2: Six-voice, first arrangement:

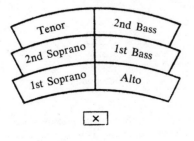

Diagram 3: Six-voice, second arrangement:

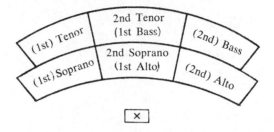

Diagram 4: Double Chorus arrangement:

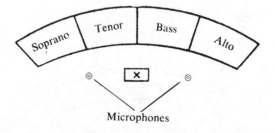

Recently there has been a tendency to use an alternate, "ray-like" arrangement which is particularly convenient for broadcasting or recording. In this arrangement one or more singers from each voice section must stand in the front row so that all parts are equidistant from the microphone or microphones. There is much to be said for this formation besides its obvious advantages for microphone use: it produces a more closely contained sound and gives the singers themselves a clearer impression of their tone.[1]

Diagram 5: Four-voice arrangement:

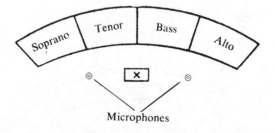

Microphones

---

[1] Mention should be made of another recent plan by which members of a four-part chorus are grouped in individual quartets. This is particularly effective for achieving independence and security in rehearsals. (Translators' note.)

Diagram 6: Double Chorus arrangement:

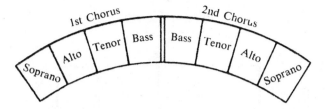

A third possible arrangement that has proved highly advantageous and is quite popular among choruses because it combines the merits of the other two arrangements is the following:

Diagram 7: Four-voice arrangement:

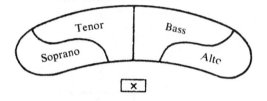

Diagram 8: Six-voice arrangement:

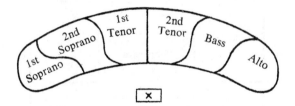

Diagram 9: Double Chorus arrangement:

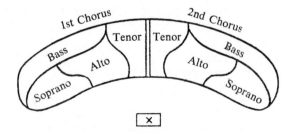

Whatever the arrangements, a circular segment—even a complete circle, the conductor forming part of it or its center—is always preferable to a rectangular formation because it enables the singers to hear each other better.

Chorus and Orchestra

Of the various possible arrangements of chorus and orchestra, the following is probably the most common as well as the most convenient:

Diagram 10:

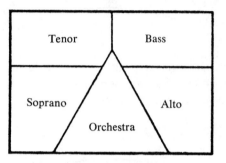

However, there are other accepted arrangements, particularly for works in which the orchestra is of superior importance, as for example Beethoven's *Ninth Symphony.*

Diagram 11:

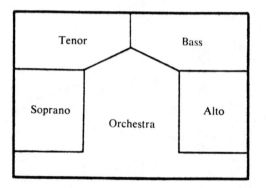

The following three arrangements are not recommended: the first, because of the complete division of the chorus segments; the second, because the chorus is too far removed from the conductor and the audience; the third, because the chorus does not have sufficient contact with the orchestra.

Diagram 12: [Three Figures]

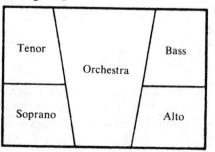

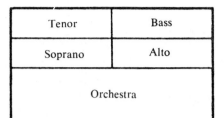

Tenor	Bass
Soprano	Alto
Orchestra	

Orchestra	
Tenor	Bass
Soprano	Alto

To all these possibilities further variants determined by space and occasion can be added; particularly works for double chorus and works employing cantus firmus and echo effects can be made much more effective through appropriate placement of the chorus.

External Factors

The chorus as a whole must present a balanced appearance: it must be symmetrically arranged on the stage and must look well.

The first principle of attire must be that *the attention of the audience should not be distracted from the work being performed.* Generally the men wear dark business suits and ties. A conglomeration of colorful dresses can lead to an appalling juxtaposition of colors. Therefore it is best that all the women wear black or at least dark dresses to achieve a unified effect. All-white attire for the women has also been used in many choruses. This produces a good visual impression particularly in large-scale performances. For small choruses, dark clothing is the most suitable.

Needless to say, before, during, and after the performance quiet and concentration must reign; the slightest murmur is out of place. An orderly entrance and exit is by no means a mere external factor, and rising and sitting during large choral works must proceed absolutely in unison, noiselessly, and quickly. These are things that every choral conductor should observe.

CHAPTER 9

General Observations on Choral Literature and Program Planning

For the first part of this chapter I am indebted to the "Guide to Choral Literature" (*Führer durch die Chorliteratur*) by Georg Schünemann which gives a comprehensive summary of this subject.[1]

Music publishers are generally willing to send copies of their publications to choral conductors for examination on approval—particularly if they know what type of chorus, program purposes, and levels of technical proficiency are involved.

The entire matter of program planning and balancing is one of the most sensitive problems the conductor faces, and one on which it is almost impossible to find uniform opinion. Much has been said and written about the question, without even approaching a solution that satisfies everyone's needs. The very need for a discussion of this subject implies a certain lack of discrimination. A program that consists of a series of unrelated numbers and a variety of musical types and contents reflects a basic lack of judgment, much like the placement of paintings in a museum without any logical order or relationship. In Kakuzo Okakura's *The Book of Tea* we learn how in Oriental culture a work of art is made the focal point of a room arrangement. Attention is focused on this one work without distraction. Then, after a certain time, the object is replaced by another, which in turn claims everyone's undivided attention. Likewise a musical composition and its individual quality claim placement in a certain framework or function. This may be, for example, at a specific point in a service of worship or in a secular concert or outdoor ceremony. All music prior to the end of the eighteenth century was written for some special occasion or purpose and thus was *Gebrauchsmusik;* this is also true to a considerable extent for music of our time. The matter is different, however, with the

---

[1] See also Erich Valentin, *Handbuch der Chormusik,* 2 vols. (Gustav Bosse Verlag, Regensburg, 1953, 1958)

works that followed the establishment of commercial concert life and that were clearly intended for performance on concert programs. Here the composer is aware of all that this situation entails—the possible success or failure of a performance, and all the external details connected with the presentation, though these may be quite subordinate to the essential quality of the music. Interestingly enough, during this period only a minimal amount of significant *a cappella* choral music was written.

One solution to the problem of program planning is to find a single choral work which will occupy the entire program. There are, however, very few extensive *a cappella* works, even for a program intended to last only an hour. Works in this category are some of the old Passion settings (Schütz), or such *a cappella* works of the twentieth century as the *Choral Passion* or the *Christmas Story* of Hugo Distler [2] or the *Saint Mark Passion* or the *Christmas Oratorio* of the author.[3] Any of these works can be taken out of the context of a service of worship and form a single program.

With a program composed of shorter works, an overall plan that takes into account contrasting elements must be apparent, and any suggestion of haphazard arrangement or disturbing juxtaposition should be avoided. Recent trends to place sacred music once again within the framework of a church service or vespers—as has been the practice for centuries in the motet concerts of the Thomanerchor, Leipzig, or the vespers of the Kreuzchor, Dresden—and to encourage the participation of the congregation, as well as the increasing number of audience participation in "open sings," show an awareness of the proper setting and function of choral music. Nevertheless, commercial concert life occupies a strong position in our culture, and it is not likely that its role will be diminished; the sheer joy of listening to music without active participation is too strong. What is to be hoped for is that concert life may undergo changes for the better.

The question remains: how should a program for a concert or church vespers be arranged? The length of a choral program, especially for an evening concert, should not exceed an hour and a half (performances of single works requiring more time are, of course, excepted). The audience should never become satiated and tired; on the contrary, the listeners should leave with the feeling that they would like to hear more.

What are the unifying elements for compiling a program? One point of departure is an historical orientation. Another is similarity of type or genre. A third is the purely artistic relationship among the different works, an approach most open to debate and subject to personal taste.

Much may be said in favor of the historical and style-oriented programs; they are sure to attain a sense of unity. The danger is that they easily become programs of purely musicological interest appealing primarily to

---

[2] Edited with an English text by Concordia Publishing House (St. Louis, Missouri).
[3] Both published by Breitkopf and Härtel, Leipzig (Wiesbaden), available from Associated Music Publishers (G. Schirmer, New York).

the specialist. One should make it a point to avoid any semblance of *l'art pour l'art;* a good program must have meaning for many listeners.

There are only a limited number of composers whose works exhibit sufficient variety to make up an entire program without boring the listener. This is possible with Bach, Handel, Schütz, Praetorius, or Lechner. If a program consists of works by various composers of the same period, particular care must be exercised in choice and order. The works selected should preferably have a common theme or subject.

I think the most plausible and intelligible programs are those built around such a subject or theme. In such a case all works chosen should have a common style or be from the same period or from different style periods which blend well. An excellent program can be made by combining sixteenth and seventeenth century choral music with twentieth century works. Combinations of seventeenth and nineteenth century or of nineteenth and twentieth century works are apt to be less successful.

The worst sort of program results from having a series of colorful and highly individualistic pieces placed one after the other but having absolutely nothing in common. The general effect of such a program is nil: each piece loses its individuality.

The matter of key relationship between pieces on a program is an important consideration. A direct sequence of pieces in totally unrelated keys will impair the flow of the program. On the other hand, several works in the same key may bore the listener. Here the solution is midway between the extremes.

It is always good to group together a number of very short pieces which are directly related to each other. This is easily done with settings based on folk melodies or on a chorale melody. With a chorale melody as cantus firmus it is possible to achieve a considerable diversity; the type of setting may be changed from verse to verse, including instrument and audience participation. The numerous settings of a single chorale melody in two, three, four and five voices by Praetorius are excellent examples. Such a group might be introduced with a chorale prelude by Samuel Scheidt, or another organ work based on the same chorale.

Each program should include one large work which is best placed at the end. For an evening vesper in which the chorus plays a major part, the final number should be a choral, not an instrumental work. A judiciously planned alternation of choral and instrumental works might have a most refreshing influence on the plan of the program. But one must be careful not to allow the instrumental sound—especially that of the organ—to stifle the effectiveness of the choral sound. The choice of instruments should depend upon the style of the choral works being sung. A piano solo in a program of Renaissance and Baroque music is obviously misplaced.

The ideal situation is, of course, that of proper balance as well as integration of vocal and instrumental forces, but a discussion of such program possibilities would exceed our present scope.

SELECTED BIBLIOGRAPHY

CONDUCTING TECHNIQUE

Finn, Fr. William J. *The Art of the Choral Conductor*. Boston: C. C. Birchard, 1939.

Finn, Fr. William J. *The Conductor Raises His Baton*. New York and London: Harper and Brothers, 1944.

Rudolf, Max. *The Grammar of Conducting*. New York: G. Schirmer, Inc., 1950.

Scherchen, Hermann. *Handbook of Conducting*. Translated by Calvocoressi. New York: Oxford University Press, 1933.

Wood, Sir Henry. *About Conducting*. London: Sylvan Press, 1945.

VOCAL TECHNIQUE

Appelman, D. Ralph. *The Science of Vocal Pedagogy: Theory and Application*. Bloomington, Indiana: Indiana University Press, 1967. (Companion album of five records.)

Kofler, Leo. *The Art of Breathing as the Basis of Tone Production*. New York, 1889, and four subsequent editions.

Marshall, Madeleine. *The Singer's Manual of English Diction*. New York: G. Schirmer, Inc., 1946.

Roma, Lisa. *The Art of Singing*. New York: G. Schirmer, Inc., 1956.

Vennard, William. *Singing, the Mechanism and Technique,* rev. enlarged ed. New York: Carl Fischer, 1967.

HISTORY and LITERATURE

Blume, Friedrich. *Geschichte der evangelischen Kirchenmusik,* 2nd enlarged ed. Kassel and Basel: Bärenreiter Verlag, 1965.

Douglas, Winfred. *Church Music in History and Practice*. Revised by L. Ellinwood. London: Faber and Faber, 1962.

Grout, Donald. *A History of Western Music*. New York: W. W. Norton, 1960.

Jacobs, Arthur, ed. *Choral Music (a Symposium)*. Baltimore: Penguin Books, 1963.

Knapp, J. Merrill. *Selected List of Music for Men's Voices*. Princeton: Princeton University Press, 1952.

Lang, Paul Henry. *Music in Western Civilization*. New York: W. W. Norton, 1941.

Locke, Arthur Ware, and Fassett, Charles. *Selected List of Choruses for Women's Voices*. 3rd ed. rev. and enlarged. Northampton, Mass.: Smith College, 1964.

Riedel, Johannes, ed. *Cantors at the Crossroads*. Saint Louis: Concordia Publishing House, 1967.

Schering, A. *Tabellen zur Musikgeschichte.* 5th ed. Edited and enlarged by Hans Joachim Moser. Wiesbaden: Breitkopf und Härtel, 1962.

Valentin, Erich. *Handbuch der Chormusik.* Regensburg: Gustav Bosse Verlag, Volume I, 1953, Volume II, 1958.

Wienandt, Elwyn A. *Choral Music of the Church.* New York: The Free Press, 1965.

Young, Percy. *The Choral Tradition.* London: Hutchinson, 1962; also in paperback, New York: W. W. Norton, 1971.

INDEX

Alfred Mann is Professor of Music at Rutgers University, Editor of the American Choral Review, and Director of the Bethlehem Bach Choir.

William H. Reese is Professor of Music at Haverford College, Conductor of the Philadelphia Chamber Chorus, and Artistic Director of several music festivals.

Acknowledgment is made to William Meads of the faculty of the University of California for his assistance in one section of the translation.